Northumberland and Durham

with North and East Yorkshire

by

F. R. BANKS

Letts Motor Tour Guides

Printed and Published by
Charles Letts & Company Limited
London, Edinburgh & New York
Head Office:
Diary House, Borough Road, London, S.E.1

Publishing Consultant: Lionel Leventhal

Cover Artist: Kenneth Farnhill

Maps: Jack Parker and Alan Walton

Northumberland and Durham
with North and East Yorkshire
by F. R. Banks
first published 1970
Standard Book Number: 85097027 X

How to use your Letts Motor Tour Guide

The best way to see Britain is, for most people, by car. This Tour Guide has been specially designed to lead you—the motorist—to all that is best in its chosen area.

Northumberland and Durham, with North and East Yorkshire

This series of tours explores the North-East of England east of the Pennines and north of the Humber, one of the least known areas of the country, yet one of the most interesting and beautiful. It includes the quiet chalklands of the Yorkshire Wolds, the heather-clad heights and charming valleys of the North Yorkshire Moors, one of our National Parks, and the great cliffs and bays of the Yorkshire Coast.

The tours also take in the historic cities of York and Durham, many other delightful towns and villages, some fascinating houses and numerous castles and ruined abbeys. They explore the courses of the Tees, the Wear, the Tyne and other fine rivers, the unique Roman wall of the Emperor Hadrian, the long and secluded strand of the Northumberland Coast, and the Border Country with its legends of ancient feuds and the lonely Cheviot Hills.

The Tours

There are ten motor tours in this guide and each tour covers a little over a hundred miles. If you wish to visit and explore all the places mentioned, you may find that a single tour will provide two or more good days' motoring. All the tours are circular, and so you can start and finish a route at any point you may choose. The book is yours to use in your own way.

The Maps

The maps (one for each tour and a larger one for the whole area) have been specially designed to show clearly all the information you will need—without being unduly technical. Readers who lack expertise in map-reading will have no difficulty in following the directions and the route. The main approach roads to the tours are also indicated.

Reference Books

For those who wish to use more detailed maps, Sheet 9 of the Ordnance Survey quarter-inch maps covers much of the area, while Sheets 7 and 11 take in the northern and southern parts respectively.

Particulars are given in the tours of the days and times of opening for houses, castles and museums, and these are correct at the time of going to press. The most recent information can be obtained from *Historic Houses, Castles and Gardens in Great Britain,* which is published annually in February. Details regarding museums and art galleries are given in *Museums and Galleries in Great Britain,* published yearly in July. The comprehensive AA Guide *Britain's Heritage,* also published annually, includes in one book information on houses, gardens and castles as well as museums and art galleries.

Particulars of hotels, restaurants and inns are given in the annual reference guide, *Hotels and Restaurants in Britain,* published by the British Travel Association. An annual selective and critical guide to eating places is Raymond Postgate's *Good Food Guide,* and a more extensive annual critical guide to hotels, restaurants, pubs and inns is written by Egon Ronay.

This Series

This Motor Tour Guide is part of a continuing series which will cover the whole of the British Isles. Other titles in this series are:

Devon and Cornwall

Somerset and Dorset, including Salisbury

Hampshire and Wiltshire, South Berks and the Isle of Wight

Kent, Surrey and Sussex

The Thames Valley, the Chilterns and Oxford

South and West Wales

Stratford and the Cotswolds, the Wye Valley

East Anglia, including Cambridge

North Wales and Anglesey

The Welsh Borders, from Hereford to Chester

The Peak District south to Stratford

The Lake District, the Pennines and Yorkshire Dales

The Scottish Lowlands and the Borders

The Highlands from Edinburgh to Inverness

The North-West Highlands and Skye

Contents

Maps

Tour Maps are on the first or second page of each tour.

Title page: *Durham Cathedral and the River Wear* (photograph: Northumberland and Durham Travel Association).

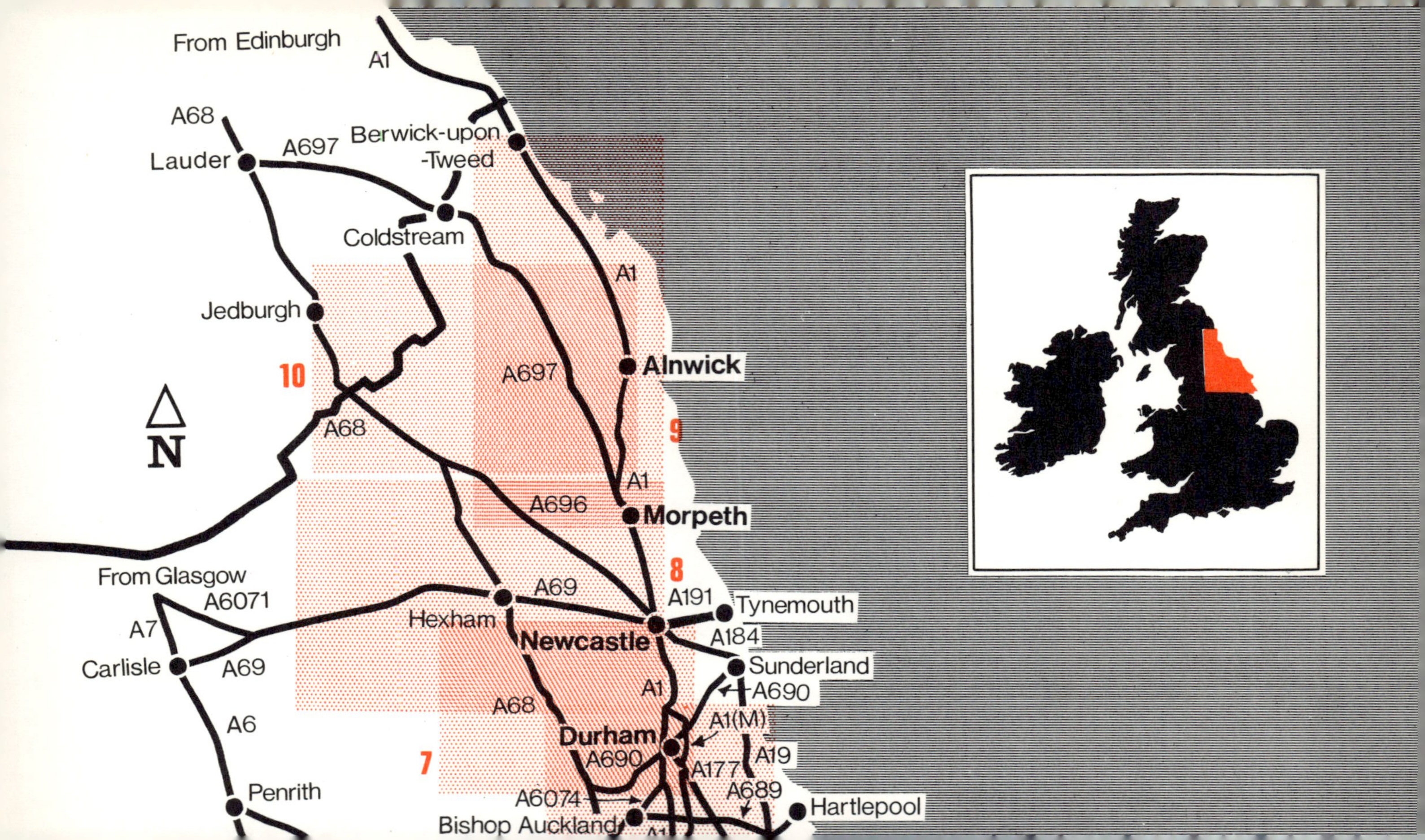
From Edinburgh
A1
A68
Berwick-upon
-Tweed
Lauder
A697
Coldstream
A1
Jedburgh
10
Alnwick
A697
A68
N
9
A1
A696
Morpeth
8
From Glasgow
A69
A6071
A191
Tynemouth
Hexham
A7
Newcastle
A184
Carlisle
A69
Sunderland
A1
A690
A68
A6
A1(M)
Durham
A19
7
A690
A177
A689
Penrith
A6074
Hartlepool
Bishop Auckland

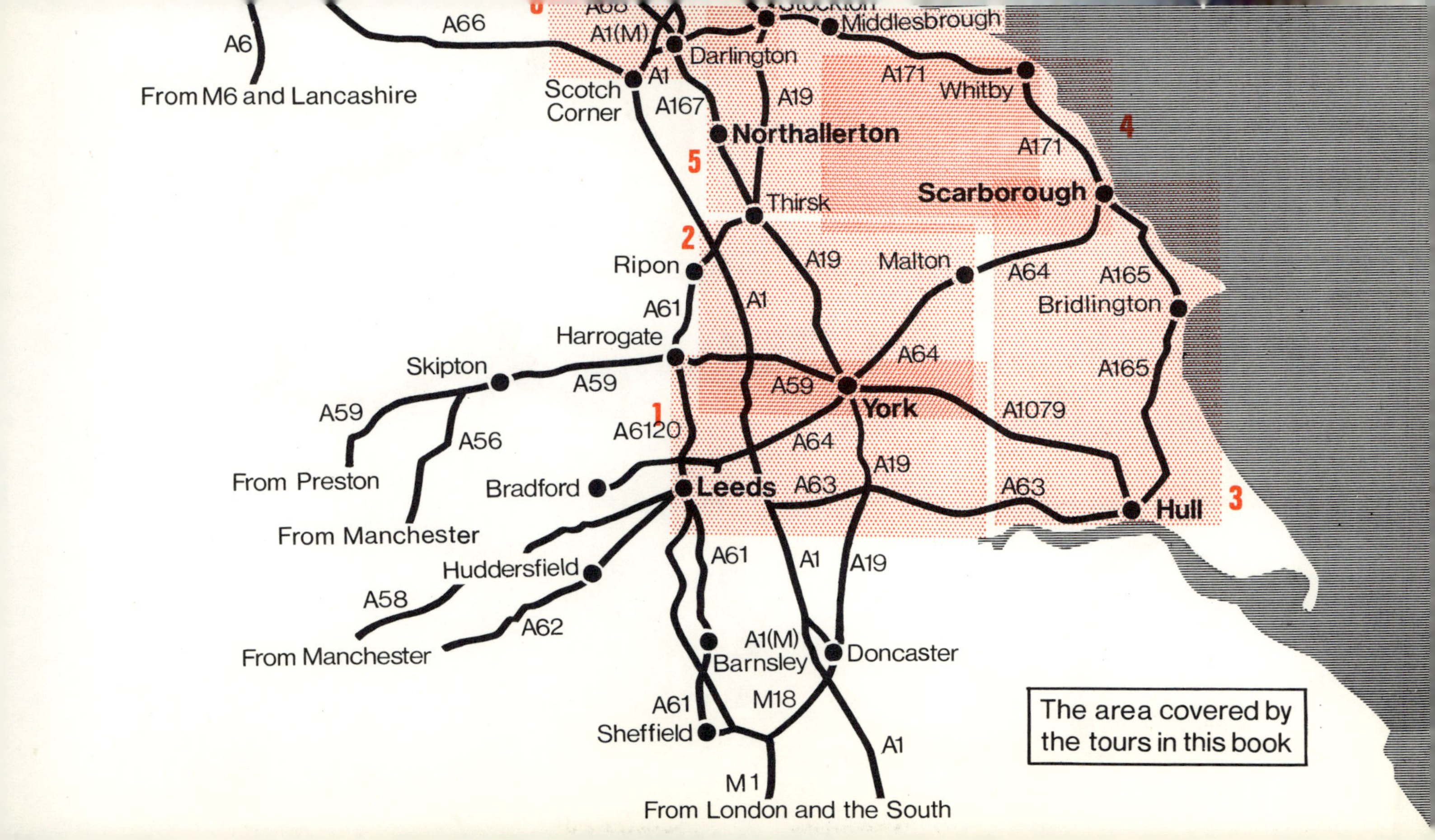
A6
From M6 and Lancashire
A66
A1(M)
Darlington
Middlesbrough
A1
Scotch Corner
A167
A19
A171
Whitby
Northallerton
5
4
A171
Scarborough
Thirsk
2
Ripon
A19
Malton
A64
A165
Bridlington
A61
A1
Harrogate
Skipton
A59
A64
A165
A59
York
1
A59
A56
A6120
A1079
A64
A19
From Preston
Bradford
Leeds
A63
A63
Hull
3
From Manchester
A61
A1
A19
Huddersfield
A58
A62
From Manchester
A1(M)
Barnsley
Doncaster
A61
M18
Sheffield
A1
M1
From London and the South
The area covered by the tours in this book

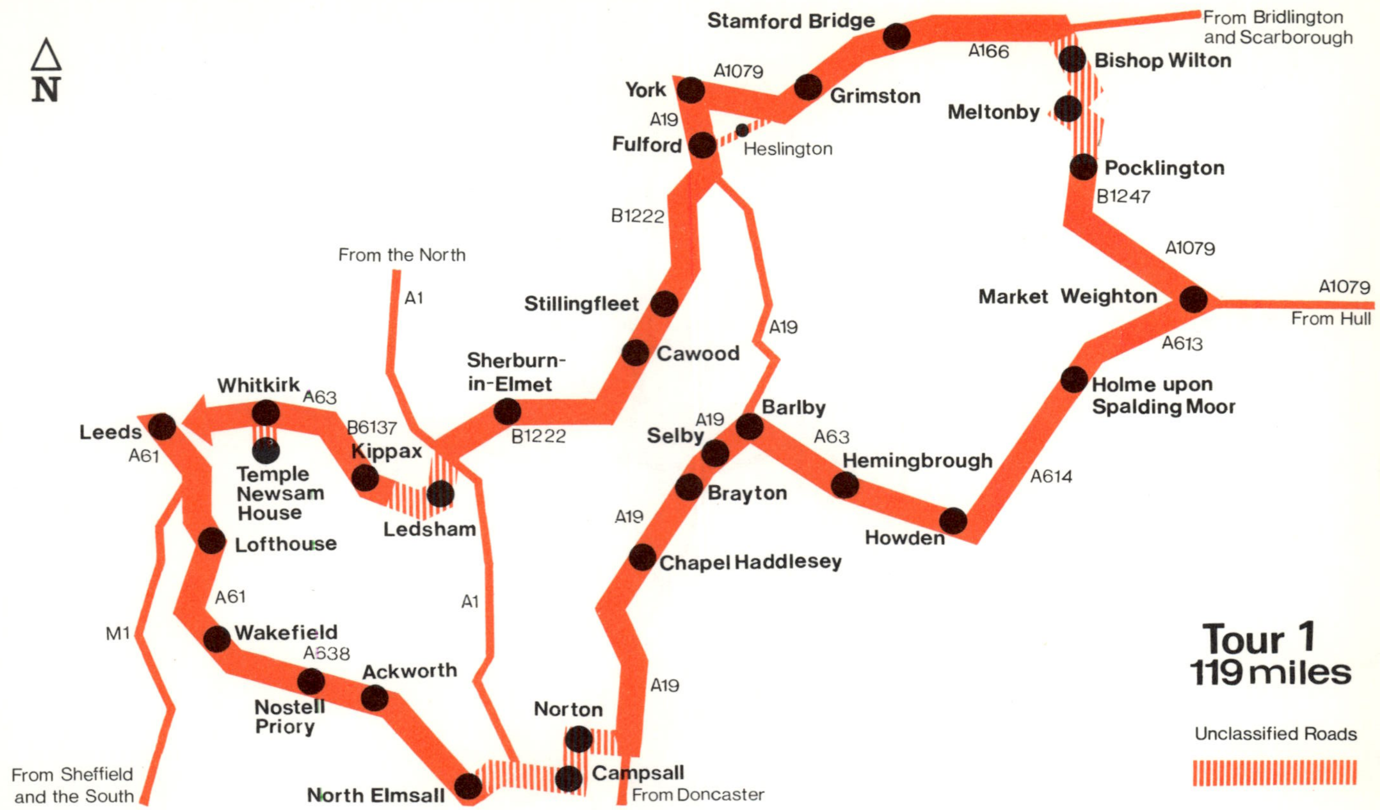
N
Stamford Bridge
From Bridlington
and Scarborough
A166
Bishop Wilton
York
A1079
Grimston
Meltonby
A19
Fulford
Heslington
Pocklington
B1247
B1222
A1079
From the North
A1
Market Weighton
A1079
From Hull
Stillingfleet
A19
A613
Cawood
Sherburn-
in-Elmet
Holme upon
Spalding Moor
Whitkirk
A63
Leeds
A61
B6137
Kippax
B1222
A19
Barlby
Selby
A63
Hemingbrough
A614
Temple
Newsam
House
Ledsham
Brayton
A19
Howden
Lofthouse
Chapel Haddlesey
A61
A1
M1
Wakefield
A638
Ackworth
A19
Nostell
Priory
Norton
From Sheffield
and the South
North Elmsall
Campsall
From Doncaster
Tour 1
119 miles
Unclassified Roads

1. The Lower Vale of York

This tour, starting from the thriving industrial city of Leeds, explores the lower part of the Vale of York, the name usually given to the fertile central plain of Yorkshire, lying between the Pennine Hills on the west and the North Yorkshire Moors and the Yorkshire Wolds on the east, and extending from the Humber and its tributary the Ouse in the south to the Tees, the boundary with County Durham. The route takes in the beautiful and historic city of York (described in Tour 2), the cathedral city of Wakefield and other old market towns such as Selby (noted for its abbey church), Market Weighton and Pocklington, near the foot of the Wolds (Tour 3). It also includes the splendid houses of Nostell Priory and Temple Newsam, charming villages such as Bishop Wilton and Stamford Bridge, and a wealth of interesting churches, of which those at Hemingbrough and Howden are outstanding.

From Leeds (City Square) east via Boar Lane, then by Briggate (right) and Hunslet Road, and on by A61 to Wakefield (9 miles).

Wakefield, on the River Calder, is the county town of the West Riding and a market and textile-manufacturing centre. The cathedral, the seat of a bishop since 1888, is a large parish church, mostly of about 1420-75 and in the Perpendicular style, but restored in 1858-74 by Sir Gilbert Scott and enlarged on the east by F. L. Pearson (1905). It has a fine tower and spire, the highest (247 feet) in Yorkshire, 15th-century stalls with misericords, and many windows of 1872-1900 by C. E. Kempe. Over the river at the foot of Kirkgate is the Bridge Chapel, the finest of the five remaining in England, built in 1342, restored by Scott in the original rich Decorated style, and refronted in 1939. In Wood Street, north-west of the cathedral, is the former Mechanics' Institute, built in 1821 and now containing the City Museum (admission weekdays 11 to 6, Sundays 2.30 to 5.30), mostly of local history, with shop and other interiors. Farther north is the City Art Gallery (admission weekdays 11 to 5, Sundays 2 to 5.30), specializing in modern art.

A61 on from Kirkgate across the river, then A638 (left) to the entrance to Nostell Priory (5½ miles).

Nostell Priory (admission Easter to early October, Wednesdays, Saturdays and Sundays, daily from August to mid-September, 2 to 6; Bank Holiday Mondays and the preceding Sundays, 11 to 6) is a delightful classical mansion begun in 1733 by James Paine and continued in 1766-80 by Robert Adam. The state rooms, superbly decorated by Adam, Joseph Rose and Antonio Zucchi, contain fine paintings (including a famous portrait of Sir Thomas More and his family by Holbein) and excellent furnishings, especially the great range of Chippendale furniture, some actually designed by Adam. In the deer park is the parish church of Wragby (1533), which has a Norman font, brought from an East Riding church submerged by the sea, 17th-18th-century pulpit panels from Italy and Germany, original glass in the east window, and nearly 500 panels and roundels of 16th-18th-century painted glass from Switzerland.

A638 on to Ackworth Moor Top (2 miles), from which Ackworth School is ½ mile north on A628.

Ackworth School (admission during the first three weeks in August, Monday-Friday, 10 to 4, by appointment) is an independent school, founded in 1779, by the Society of Friends. The older buildings, (about 1749), housed the London Foundling Hospital from 1757.

A638 on to North Elmsall (3½ miles), in a colliery district, then by an unclassified road (left, beyond the church) to Barnsdale Bar (2½ miles), where the A1 is crossed, and on to Campsall (2 miles).

Campsall is an attractive village whose church, mainly of the 13th-15th centuries, has a fine Norman tower and a tall 15th-century rood-screen.

Unclassified road north to Norton (1 mile), then east for 1½ miles more, then A19 left, crossing the Aire to Brayton (10½ miles).

Brayton has a church, mostly of the 14th and 15th centuries, with fine Norman work in the tower, south doorway and chancel arch.

A19 on to Selby (1½ miles).

Selby is a brick-built agricultural town and inland port on the south bank of the tidal Ouse, which is crossed by a wooden toll-bridge of 1791 (see below). Facing the wide market place is the magnificent abbey church, the survival of a Benedictine abbey founded about 1070. The north porch and the west front both enclose late-Norman doorways of about 1170; the east bays of the nave, the crossing tower arches and part of the north transept are Norman work of before 1123. The west end of the nave is in the Transitional Norman style (about 1200) and the south triforium and both clerestories are pure Early English work of about 1225. The beautiful choir, built in 1280-1340, has notable sedilia of about 1380 attributed to Henry Yevele. The Washington arms appear in a window of the south choir clerestory; the great 'Jesse' window of about 1340 at the east end has rich flamboyant tracery.

A19 on over the toll-bridge, entering the East Riding, for Barlby (1½ miles), then A63 (right) to Hemingbrough (3½ miles).

Hemingbrough has an excellent collegiate church of the late-12th century and later, with interesting woodwork and a 15th-century tower and needle-like spire, 180 feet high, a prominent landmark over the surrounding cornfields of the lower Ouse levels.

A63 to Loftsome Bridge (2 miles) and on 3 miles to Howden.

Howden is a small agricultural town with a splendid collegiate church, almost wholly of the 14th century. The west front is full of interesting detail; the beautiful chancel, in the mature Decorated style, and the lovely 15th-century chapter house are now in ruins. The Perpendicular tower, 135 feet high, is a distinctive landmark.

A614 left, beyond Howden, crossing level country to Holme upon Spalding Moor (8 miles), then A613 (right).

Holme upon Spalding Moor has a 13th-15th-century church, with a fine 15th-century tower, crowning a knoll from which extensive views open to the Yorkshire Wolds, the Pennines and the North Yorkshire Moors.

A613 on to Market Weighton (4½ miles).

Market Weighton is a small town with flourishing cattle and corn markets, at the foot of the escarpment of the Wolds.

A1079 left (east) for 5½ miles, then B1247 (right; see below) to Pocklington (1½ miles).

Pocklington is a charming small market town below the escarpment of the Wolds. At Pocklington School, founded in 1514 as a grammar school, William Wilberforce, the abolitionist, was a pupil. Burnby Hall Gardens (admission April-September, daily, 2-6), near B1247, include a fine water-lily pond in the grounds, while the Stewart Collection contains exhibits from all parts of the world.

Unclassified road north, below the Wolds, bearing left in 1 mile for Meltonby (1½ miles more), then right for Bishop Wilton (2 miles farther).

Bishop Wilton is a delightful brick-built village lining a wide green, at the foot of a wooded section of the Wolds. The church, though too zealously restored, has a Norman chancel arch and south doorway and a 14th-century tower and spire. the steep Garrowby Hill (see below) rises to the highest point on the Wolds (807 feet).

Unclassified road on (north) to Garrowby Hill (1 mile), then A166 left to Stamford Bridge (5 miles more).

Stamford Bridge is an attractive brick-built village on the Derwent, which is crossed by a bridge of 1727. A memorial stone near the bridge marks the site of the tremendous battle of September, 1066, in which Harold II soundly defeated the invading forces of his brother Tostig and Harald Hardraada, King of Norway, only to be defeated himself next month by the invading William of Normandy.

A166 on to Grimston (5½ miles), then A1079 on again for ½ mile, where an unclassified road branches left for Heslington (1 mile).

Heslington has a restored Elizabethan hall, now the administrative centre of the University of York, which was opened in 1963. The first colleges in the park were completed in 1965 and the Central Library in 1966, and other new buildings to be designed by Robert Matthew, Johnson-Marshall and Partners are to include a sports centre, a theatre and a concert hall. The unclassified road goes on from Heslington to reach A19 at Fulford (1 mile; see below).

A1079 on to York (3 miles from Grimston).

York is described in Tour 2 (page 13).

A19 south, leaving York by Fishergate, to Fulford (2 miles; see above) and thence to Water Fulford (½ mile), then B1222 (right) via Naburn to Stillingfleet (5 miles more).

Stillingfleet is a village bordering a large green near the Ouse. The church, partly of the 13th and 14th centuries, has a magnificent Norman south doorway with 12th-century ironwork showing Viking influence.

B1222 on, crossing the Ouse to Cawood (3 miles).

Cawood, in the West Riding, is another attractive brick-built village and has the 15th-century gatehouse of the palace of the archbishops of York, where Cardinal Wolsey was arrested in 1530.

B1222 on to Sherburn-in-Elmet (6 miles).

Sherburn-in-Elmet has a fine church (to the west of A162) with Norman, Early English and Perpendicular work. In the south aisle are the two sides of a rare 15th-century cross-head, which were divided after it was rediscovered about 1850.

B1222 on for 2½ miles, then A1 right and by an unclassified road left to Ledsham (1½ miles).

Ledsham is a secluded village whose church has much Saxon work and interesting 17th-18th-century monuments. Ledston Hall (see below) is an imposing mansion mostly of the 17th century.

Unclassified road on (west) for 1 mile, then right, passing north of Ledston Hall to reach A656 (1½ miles more); then B6137 on to Kippax (1 mile).

Kippax, a village now growing into a dormitory for Leeds, has a church with a late-Saxon or early-Norman fabric.

B6137 on for 1½ miles, then A63 (left) to Whitkirk (3 miles more), where the road for Temple Newsam (1 mile farther) branches left.

Temple Newsam House (open daily, 10.30 to 6.15 or dusk, on Wednesdays in May-September to 8.30), the birthplace in 1545 of Lord Darnley, second husband of Mary, Queen of Scots, was largely rebuilt in 1622-36. It was sold in 1922 (with the delightful grounds) to Leeds, and contains paintings (mostly British), porcelain, etc,. from the city's collection. The Great Hall has 16th-17th-century furniture, and other rooms contain English satinwood furniture, jewelled snuff-boxes and Chinese carvings in semi-precious stones. The Gallery in the north wing is 108 feet long; in the west wing are 16th-century rooms and exquisite examples of 18th-century decoration.

A63 on from Whitkirk, joining A64 in 1½ miles and reaching Leeds (the Headrow; 2½ miles more) by New York Road, Quarry Hill and Eastgate.

2. From York to the Hambleton Hills

This tour starts from the fascinating old city of York, famous for its minster and the many other historic buildings in its narrow streets. The route crosses the rich, fertile country of the Vale of York towards the Howardian Hills, a wooded limestone range which faces the Wolds across the Vale of the Derwent, and goes on to the Hambleton Hills, the western buttress of the North Yorkshire Moors (Tour 4). The tour takes in some delightful villages and interesting churches, the old market towns of Malton, Thirsk, Boroughbridge and Knaresborough, the Roman remains at Aldborough, the medieval remains of Kirkham Priory and Spofforth Castle, and a variety of fine houses, such as the magnificent Castle Howard, Nunnington Hall, Rudding Park and Bramham Park.

York, on the River Ouse, is a city of the greatest historic interest, with a great many old buildings and restricted streets retaining their medieval appearance. It is still almost completely enclosed by its City Walls, among the finest examples in Europe of medieval town fortification, mainly of the 14th century, but following the line of their Roman forerunners in the north-west angle. The minster, the seat of the Archbishop of York and the largest medieval cathedral in England, has 13th-century transepts, a 14th-century nave with a magnificent west front, and a 15th-century choir and towers, including the great central tower, the largest in England. It has also a beautiful 14th-century chapter house and a superb range of medieval stained glass windows, among them the 13th-century Five Sisters window in the north transept and the great east window of about 1400 by John Thornton of Coventry. Noteworthy glass is to be seen, too, in St. Michael-le-Belfrey, Holy Trinity and others of the many interesting churches in York. St. William's College (admission weekdays to dusk), east of the minster, is a restored Jacobean building, partly timber-framed, and the Treasurer's House (admission weekdays, March-November, 11 to 4 or 6; Sundays, June-September, 11 to 6), close by, is a delightful 17th-century stone building with interesting furniture. The Museum Gardens, bordering the Ouse, contain the 13th-century ruins of St. Mary's Abbey and the Yorkshire Museum (admission weekdays, 10 to 5), with collections of antiquities and natural history. The City Art Gallery (admission weekdays, 10 to 5; Sundays 2.30 to 5), outside Bootham Bar, one of the fine city gates, has an excellent collection of European and English paintings. Among the 18th-century buildings are the Assembly Rooms, in Blake Street, and the Mansion House, in St. Helen's Square. The 15th-century Guildhall, beside the river, has been partly rebuilt after its gutting by bombing; in Piccadilly, some distance east, is the Merchant Adventurers' Hall (admission weekdays, 10 to 12.30 and 2 to 4, 5 or 6; closed Mondays in winter),

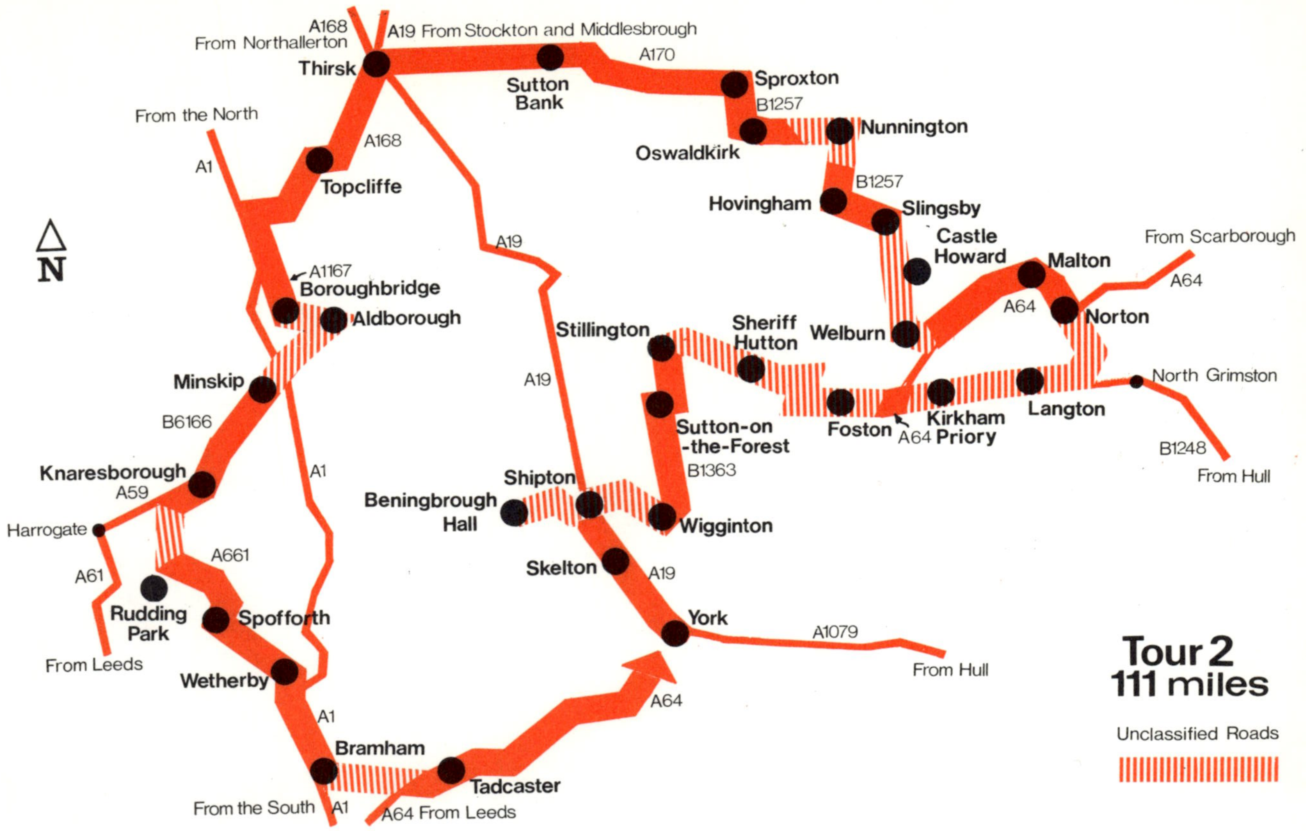

Tour 2
111 miles
Unclassified Roads
N
A168
From Northallerton
A19 From Stockton and Middlesbrough
Thirsk
Sutton
Bank
A170
Sproxton
B1257
Nunnington
Oswaldkirk
B1257
Hovingham
Slingsby
Castle
Howard
Malton
From Scarborough
A64
A64
Norton
Welburn
Sheriff
Hutton
Stillington
North Grimston
Foston
A64
Kirkham
Priory
Langton
B1248
From Hull
From the North
A1
A168
Topcliffe
A19
A1167
Boroughbridge
Aldborough
Minskip
B6166
A19
Sutton-on
-the-Forest
B1363
Knaresborough
A59
A1
Shipton
Beningbrough
Hall
Wigginton
Harrogate
A61
A661
Skelton
A19
Rudding
Park
Spofforth
York
A1079
From Hull
From Leeds
Wetherby
A64
A1
Bramham
Tadcaster
From the South
A1
A64 From Leeds

which is mainly of the 14th and 15th centuries. Of the two castles founded by William the Conqueror, the Norman motte of one supports the unusual 14th-century Clifford's Tower (admission 9.30 to 4, 5.30 or 7; closed Sundays to 2 in winter). The absorbing Castle Museum (admission weekdays, 9.30 to 4.30 or 7.30; Sundays from 2) has old 'bygones' and a reconstructed street of 18th-19th-century shops. To the south of the river is an interesting Railway Museum (admission weekdays, 10 to 5) containing a unique collection of old engines and rolling stock.

A19, leaving York by Bootham and Clifton, through the Vale of York to Skelton (3½ miles).

Skelton, an attractive village embowered in trees, has a small but complete Early English church, built about 1247.

A19 on to Shipton (2 miles), from which a by-road leads left to Beningbrough Hall (2½ miles more).

Beningbrough Hall (admission April-September, Wednesdays and Saturdays, 2 to 6 or dusk), in a pleasant wooded park near the Ouse, was built in 1716, possibly by Thomas Archer, and has fine interior decoration.

Unclassified road right (east) from Shipton to Wigginton (2½ miles), then B1363 (left) to Sutton-on-the-Forest (4 miles more).

Sutton-on-the-Forest (i.e., the former royal forest of Galtres) borders a long green and has a rebuilt church containing an 18th-century pulpit from which Laurence Sterne preached. The vicarage replaces that in which Sterne lived from 1738 until 1760 (when he moved to Coxwold) and in which he began *Tristram Shandy*.

B1363 on to Stillington (2 miles), then by an unclassified road (right) via Farlington to Sheriff Hutton (4½ miles farther).

Sheriff Hutton is strikingly placed on a ridge with a view over the Vale of York. The ruins of the castle, a 14th-century stronghold of the Nevilles, rise dramatically at the west end of the village; at the other end is the church, mostly of the 14th and 15th centuries, with a restored tomb which has an effigy said to be that of Edward, the only child of Richard III.

Unclassified road on (east), bearing right in 1½ miles and left in 1 mile farther, to Thornton-le-Clay (1 mile more) and thence to Foston (1 mile).

Foston has a rectory (just east of Thornton-le-Clay) rebuilt in 1814 by Sydney Smith, the author and wit, who was rector here, and a church with a good Norman south doorway and chancel arch.

Unclassified road on to Whitwell-on-the-Hill (1½ miles), above the wooded Derwent Valley, then A64 (left) and by an unclassified road (right) across the river to Kirkham Priory (½ mile).

Kirkham Priory (admission weekdays, 9.30 to 4, 5.30 or 7; Sundays from 2), in the East Riding, was founded after 1122 for Augustinian canons. The principal remains are the late-13th-century gatehouse and part of the cloister, with a vaulted entrance and a beautiful 13th-century lavatorium.

Unclassified road on, branching left in ½ mile, to Langton (4 miles farther).

Langton is a well-kept village with grey stone cottages, below the escarpment of the Yorkshire Wolds. Langton Wold, to the north, is a noted racehorse training ground.

Unclassified road on for 1 mile, then left, crossing Langton Wold, to Norton (3 miles more; see below); then A64 (left), crossing the Derwent to Malton (½ mile).

Malton, in the North Riding, is a thriving agricultural town with interesting stone houses of the 17th and 18th centuries, among them the Talbot Hotel. The museum (admission Monday to Friday on application to the Town Hall; Sundays in July and August, 2 to 5), near the broad sloping Market Place, contains finds from the near-by Roman settlement of *Derventio*. At Old Malton, to the north-east on A169, the church preserves 15th-century and earlier remains of a Gilbertine priory founded about 1150. Norton (see above) has been a racehorse training centre since 1736.

A64 south-west for 4½ miles, then by an unclassified road (right) through Welburn (1 mile), then right again ½ mile farther on, through an avenue of limes and beeches, for Castle Howard (1½ miles more).

Castle Howard (admission Easter to early October, Tuesdays to Thursdays, Saturdays and Sundays, 1.30 to 5; Bank Holiday Mondays 11.30 to 5.30), the magnificent classical mansion of the Howard family, was the first work of Sir John Vanbrugh, who was assisted by Nicholas Hawksmoor. Begun in 1699 for the 3rd Earl of Carlisle, the imposing hall, 70 feet high, was finished about 1710 and the south front and east wing by 1714. The west wing, with the long gallery, was added in 1759 by Sir Thomas Robinson. The house is famous for its art collection, which includes paintings by Holbein, Rubens, Van Dyck, Reynolds, Romney and Gainsborough. In the stables an excellent museum of 18th-20th-century costumes has been arranged. The beautiful park contains a large lake and many fine landscape buildings.

Unclassified road on through the avenue to Slingsby (3 miles), then B1257 (left) to Hovingham (2 miles).

Slingsby and Hovingham are described in Tour 5 (page 33).

B1257 on for 1½ miles, then by an unclassified road on to Nunnington (1 mile).

Nunnington, a village on the Rye, which flows through the Vale of Pickering (Tour 4), has a large 16th-17th-century hall (admission May-September, Wednesdays and Sundays, 2 to 6).

Unclassified road left (west) for 2 miles, then B1257 again (right) to Oswaldkirk (1 mile; Tour 5) and thence to Sproxton (2 miles more); then A170 (left), ascending over the Hambleton Hills to the top of Sutton Bank (6½ miles farther).

Sutton Bank is a precipitous descent on the face of the Hambleton Hills (981 feet), with an extensive view from the top over the Vale of York to the Pennines beyond. To the north is the limestone crag of Whitestone Cliff (1064 feet); to the south, towards Roulston Scar (Tour 5), is the flying-ground of the Yorkshire Gliding Club. Below the escarpment is the small wood-enclosed lake of Gormire, which has no visible feeder or outlet.

A170 on, descending Sutton Bank (gradient 1 in 4; care required) to Sutton-under-Whitestonecliffe (2½ miles) and thence to Thirsk (3½ miles more).

Thirsk is a busy agricultural town in the upper Vale of York, with 18th-century houses and inns round the large cobbled market place and in Kirkgate. This leads to the magnificent 15th-century church, which has excellent carved roofs in the nave and aisles.

A168 south-west to Topcliffe (4½ miles).

Topcliffe, an old-world village on the Swale, has a church, rebuilt in the Decorated style in 1855, with a splendid 14th-century brass of Flemish workmanship.

A168 on for 3½ miles, then A1 (left) for 2 miles to the Boroughbridge by-pass; then A1167 (left again) to Boroughbridge (2 miles).

Boroughbridge is a small town, once a busy coaching stage, with several attractive old inns, on the south bank of the Ure, in the West Riding. The Devil's Arrows, to the west, are three huge gritstone monoliths, about 20 feet high, probably of the Bronze Age.

Unclassified road left (east) from the market place to Aldborough (1 mile).

Aldborough is a village on the site of the Roman town of *Isurium,* the cantonal capital of the Brigantes, a pre-Roman Celtic people. The visible remains are to the south-west of the 14th-15th-century church and behind the museum (admission 9.30 to 4, 5.30 or 7; Sundays from 2) and the Aldburgh Arms Inn, where there are two tessellated pavements.

Unclassified road south-west, crossing the A1 to Minskip (1½ miles), then B6166 to Knaresborough (5½ miles).

Knaresborough is an old market town, with many fine 18th-century houses, strikingly situated on a cliff high above the Nidd, which flows through a deep ravine. In a public park are the remains of John of Gaunt's Castle, where Richard II was imprisoned in 1399. The most notable part is the 14th-century keep, which served also as a gatehouse. The large 13th-15th-century church, north of the prominent railway viaduct, has good 17th-century monuments of the Slingsby family. Near the river, upstream, is the 18th-century Conyngham Hall, which has charming grounds with a zoo. From the High Bridge a path follows the river down to the Dropping Well, noted for its petrifying properties, and Mother Shipton's Cave, near by.

A59 on south-west, crossing the Nidd to Forest Lane Head (1 mile), then by an unclassified road to reach A661 in 1½ miles farther, opposite a road which goes on to Rudding Park (1 mile more). [A59 goes on to Harrogate, in Letts Motor Tour Guide to *The Lake District and the Pennines*.]

Rudding Park (admission Easter to early October, daily, except Fridays, 2 to 6; Bank Holidays, Sunday and Monday, 11 to 7) is a delightful Regency house built in 1805-24.

A661 left (south-east) to Spofforth (3 miles).

Spofforth has a ruined 13th-15th-century castle (admission weekdays, 9.30 to 4, 5.30 or 7; Sundays from 2) of the Percy family, with a ground floor partly fashioned by the rock on which it is built.

A661 on to Wetherby (3½ miles).

Wetherby is an old market town and former coaching station on the Wharfe, which is crossed by a fine bridge, partly medieval.

A1 south, beyond the Wharfe, to Bramham (3½ miles; by-pass).

Bramham is an attractive stone-built village near the entrance to Bramham Park (admission Easter to September, Sundays and Bank Holiday Mondays and Tuesdays, 2 to 6), over a mile south-west, built in 1698, possibly by Giacomo Leoni, and standing in beautiful gardens laid out in the French style in the early 18th century.

Unclassified road east from Bramham for 2½ miles, then A64 on to Tadcaster (1½ miles).

Tadcaster, on the Wharfe, which is crossed by an 18th-century bridge, is a pleasant old town, dominated by a large brewery. The church, rebuilt in 1877 using old material, has fine glass by William Morris in the east window.

A64 on to York (9½ miles), which is entered on the south-west by Tadcaster Road.

3. The Yorkshire Wolds and Coast

This tour, starting from the busy industrial town and seaport of Kingston upon Hull, on the broad Humber, explores the Yorkshire Wolds, part of the great chalk belt which stretches across England from Dorset and breaks down to the sea in the upstanding cliffs of Flamborough Head. These open, breezy chalklands show a bold escarpment on the west and north to the Vales of York and Pickering, and on the east they enclose the vast Plain of Holderness. The route takes in the county town of Beverley, with its splendid minster, charming villages such as Bishop Burton, Weaverthorpe and Hunmanby, a variety of old churches, from Goodmanham and Kirkburn to South Dalton, the fine houses of Burton Agnes, Sledmere House and Sewerby Hall, and not least the popular coastal resorts of Scarborough (with an interesting castle on its headland), Filey and Bridlington.

From Hull (Queen Victoria Square) by King Edward Street, Prospect Street, Beverley Road and A1079 to Beverley (8 miles).

Beverley, the county town of the East Riding, is a thriving market centre with attractive 18th-century houses. The minster, mostly of the 13th and 14th centuries, is one of the most beautiful churches in England and the superior of many cathedrals. Notable features are the west façade with its twin towers, the rare double transepts, the 16th-century wood-carving of the choir stalls, and the richly sculptured 14th-century Percy tomb. In the Saturday Market, some distance north, is the distinctive 18th-century market cross, and near by is St. Mary's Church, a fine 14th-15th-century church that suffers only by comparison with the minster, and the restored brick North Bar, the only survivor of the five town gates.

A1079 on, passing the racecourse, to Bishop Burton (3 miles).

Bishop Burton, a centre of racehorse training, is an enchanting village built round a pond and a green, in a secluded wooded hollow of the Wolds.

A1079 on over the Wolds to Market Weighton (7½ miles).

Market Weighton is described in Tour 1 (page 11).

A163 north for ¼ mile, then by an unclassified road (right), ascending to Goodmanham (1¼ miles more).

Goodmanham, the Godmunddingaham of the Venerable Bede (c. 673-735), has an interesting 12th-13th-century church with two fonts, one Norman or possibly Saxon, the other of the 16th century and elaborately carved.

Unclassified road on over the open Wolds for 2½ miles, then right for 2 miles, passing north of Kipling Cotes station (see page 21), then left to South Dalton (2 miles more).

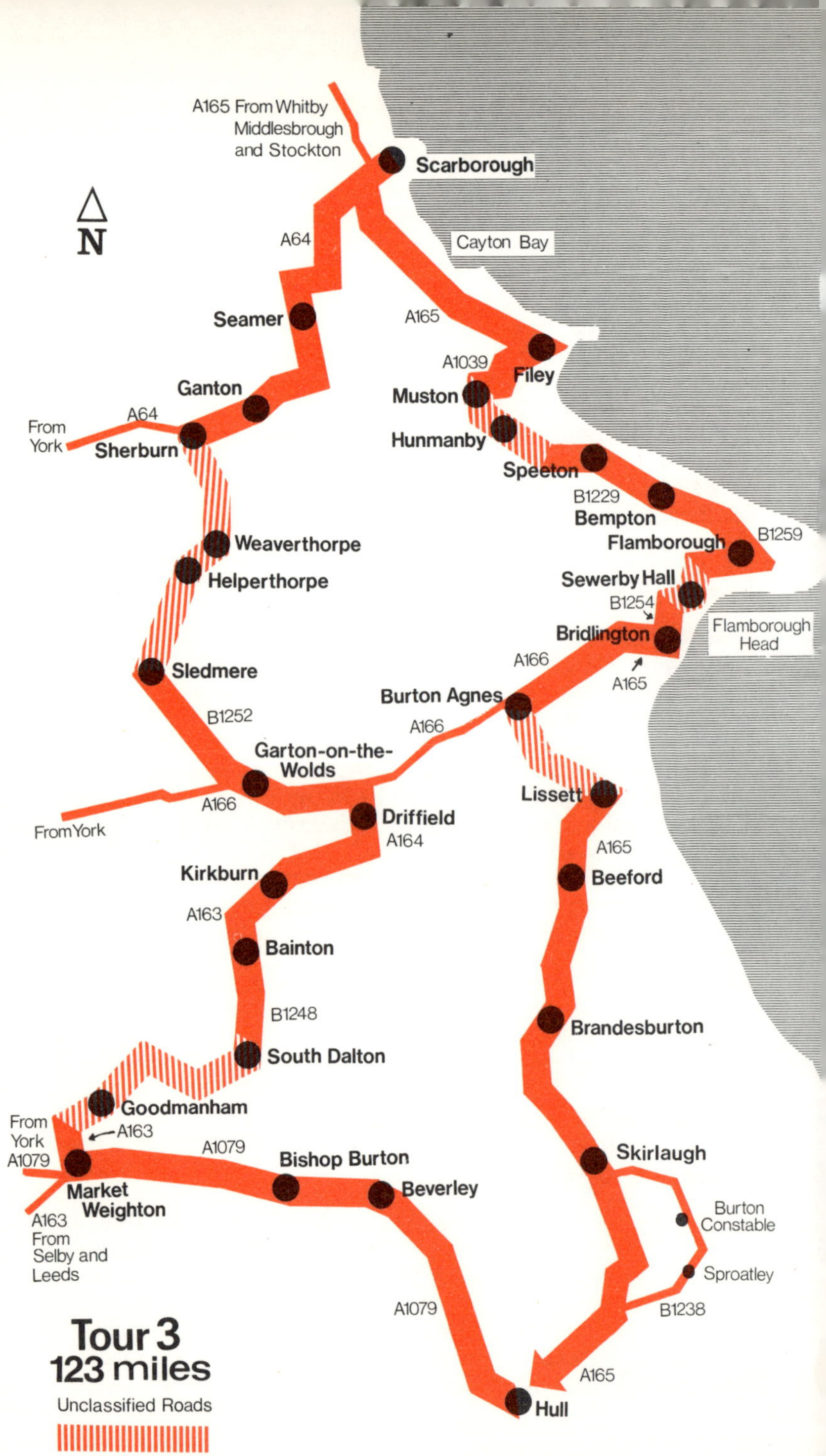

A165 From Whitby
Middlesbrough
and Stockton
Scarborough
N
A64
Cayton Bay
A165
Seamer
A1039
Filey
Muston
Ganton
A64
From
York
Sherburn
Hunmanby
Speeton
B1229
Bempton
Flamborough
B1259
Weaverthorpe
Helperthorpe
Sewerby Hall
B1254
Flamborough
Head
Bridlington
A166
A165
Sledmere
Burton Agnes
B1252
A166
Garton-on-the-
Wolds
Lissett
A166
From York
Driffield
A164
A165
Kirkburn
Beeford
A163
Bainton
B1248
Brandesburton
South Dalton
Goodmanham
From
York
A1079
A163
A1079
Bishop Burton
Skirlaugh
Market
Weighton
Beverley
Burton
Constable
A163
From
Selby and
Leeds
Sproatley
A1079
B1238
Tour 3
123 miles
A165
Hull
Unclassified Roads

South Dalton is an attractive village with a beautiful church in the Decorated style, designed by J. L. Pearson in 1858, containing the 17th-century monument of Sir John Hotham, excellent workmanship of Italian origin. Kipling Cotes is the starting-point (at midday on the third Thursday in March) of the longest (4 miles) and perhaps the oldest horse-race in England, first run in 1519.

Unclassified road north to Holme-on-the-Wolds (½ mile), then right for ½ mile more; then B1248 (left) to join A163 before reaching Bainton (3½ miles farther).

Bainton has a fine church of about 1335, completely in the Decorated style, with the interesting tomb of Sir Edmund de Mauley, who fell at Bannockburn (1314).

A163 on to Kirkburn (2 miles; on the left).

Kirkburn has a church of unusual interest, mainly Norman, with a tower containing a unique staircase of about 1200 and a chancel rebuilt in the Norman style in 1856 by Pearson.

A163 on for 3 miles, then A164 (left) to Driffield (1 mile).

Driffield is a thriving agricultural town with old houses and important corn and cattle markets. The church is basically of the 13th century, but has fine 14th-century windows and a stately 15th-century tower.

A166 west through Garton-on-the-Wolds (3 miles), then B1252 on to Sledmere (4½ miles more).

Sledmere is a model 18th-century village in a region of the Wolds whose agricultural development was pioneered by the Sykes family, who have lived since 1748 at Sledmere House (admission Sundays from Easter, Bank Holiday Mondays, and daily, except Mondays and Fridays, in May-September, 1.30 to 5.30). The house, built in 1751, enlarged in 1776-87 and altered after a fire in 1911, has fine plasterwork, furniture and family portraits. There are extensive lawns with water basins and fountains, beyond which is the beautifully wooded park, laid out by 'Capability' Brown (see page 50), and the pink-sandstone church, rebuilt in 1898 by Temple Moore.

Unclassified road north, over the Wolds, to Helperthorpe (3½ miles), then east (right) to Weaverthorpe (1 mile).

Weaverthorpe, one of several unspoilt villages in the valley of the Gypsey Race (an intermittent stream), has a well-restored church with a Saxon or early-Norman nave and tower, an early-Norman font and a Saxon sundial on the south doorway.

Unclassified road north, descending the escarpment of the Wolds to Sherburn (4 miles), then A64 (right) to Ganton (2 miles).

Ganton is an attractive village with whitewashed cottages, roofed with red pantiles, at the foot of the Wolds, with a view over the Vale of Pickering to the North Yorkshire Moors.

A64 on for 2½ miles, then left across the levels of the vale to Seamer (2½ miles more).

Seamer, in the North Riding, has an interesting Norman and 15th-century church.

A64 on to Scarborough (4½ miles), which is entered by Falsgrave Road and Westborough.

Scarborough is described in Tour 4 (page 25).

A165 south from the station, via Valley Bridge and Filey Road, passing approaches to Oliver's Mount, to Cayton Bay (2½ miles) and on for 3½ miles more, then A1039 (left) to Filey (1½ miles).

Filey is a quiet golfing and bathing resort on Filey Bay, whose sandy beach extends north to Filey Brigg, a rocky spit over ¼ mile long. The pleasant Norman and 13th-century parish church stands on the edge of a ravine.

A1039 on for 1 mile, then A165 (right) and A1039 again (left) to Muston (½ mile more); then by an unclassified road (left) to Hunmanby (1½ miles farther).

Hunmanby is an old market village pleasantly situated below the Wolds. The church, partly of the 12th-15th centuries, contains memorials of the Osbaldeston family, with unusual heraldry.

Unclassified road on, south-east, to the Dotterel Inn (3 miles; on A165), then B1229 (left) to Speeton (1 mile on the left).

Speeton, above the north escarpment of the Wolds, is noted for its gleaming chalk cliffs (400 feet high), which are extended east by Bempton Cliffs towards Flamborough Head. They are the breeding-places of innumerable sea-birds, the eggs of which used to be collected by intrepid fowlers lowered down over the precipitous cliffs on ropes.

B1229 on to Bempton (3½ miles) and thence to Flamborough (3 miles).

Flamborough is a large village whose restored church has a rare 15th-century rood-screen and loft. B1259 (busy in summer) runs east for nearly 2 miles to Flamborough Head, a bold chalk promontory where the Wolds reach their extremity. The finest scenery, with caves and rock stacks, in on the north side, towards the sandy cove of the North Landing, reached from Flamborough by B1255.

B1255 west from Flamborough, crossing the Dane's Dyke (1 mile), of pre-Roman origin, and on for 1 mile more, then by an unclassified road (left) to Sewerby Hall (½ mile).

Sewerby Hall (admission Easter-September, 10 to 12.30 and 1.30 to 6, except Saturday mornings) is an early-18th-century mansion with an art gallery, in a pleasant public park overlooking Bridlington Bay. A small zoo and deer paddock have recently been added.

Unclassified road on for 1 mile, then B1254 (left) to Bridlington (1 mile more).

Bridlington is a popular seaside resort with fine sands and a fishing and yachting harbour, on the broad curve of Bridlington Bay. In the old town, 1 mile north by A1038, are the impressive 13th-15th-century nave and west front of the priory church, approached through the massive 14th-century Bayle Gate.

A165 west from the harbour for 1½ miles, then A166 (left) to Burton Agnes (4½ miles more).

Burton Agnes has a church of the late-12th and 16th centuries with interesting monuments to the Griffith family. Burton Agnes Hall (admission May to mid-October, weekdays, except Saturdays, 1.45 to 5; Sundays, 1.45 to 6), approached through a fine gatehouse of 1610, is a charming Elizabethan manor house begun in 1601 for the Griffiths and attributed to Robert Smythson. It has richly carved chimney-pieces and panelling and an unusual oak staircase as well as a fine collection of modern French paintings. The Norman Old Manor House (always open), close by, was heightened in the 15th century and later encased in brick.

Unclassified road south to Gransmoor (3 miles) and thence to Lissett (2 miles), then A165 (right) to Beeford (2½ miles more).

Beeford, on the corn-growing plain of Holderness, has a 15th-century church with a good tower and two unusual monuments to priests.

A165 on to Brandesburton (4 miles).

Brandesburton is an old-world Holderness village with a 13th-15th-century church containing fine 14th-century brasses.

A165 on via Leven and Long Riston to Skirlaugh (6½ miles).

Skirlaugh has a remarkable chapel built about 1403 by Walter Skirlaw, Bishop of Durham. An unclassified road runs south-east for 5 miles via Marton to Burton Constable (admission Easter to late September, daily except Mondays and Fridays and including Bank Holiday Mondays, 12 to 6), the seat of the Constable family for nearly 900 years, a splendid Elizabethan mansion rebuilt about 1570 and altered in the 18th century, with notable paintings and furniture.

A165 may be regained via Sproatley, to the south, and B1238, running west to Bilton (5 miles). A165 on from Skirlaugh, passing west of Bilton (4½ miles), to Hull (4½ miles more), which is entered by Holderness Road and Clarence Street.

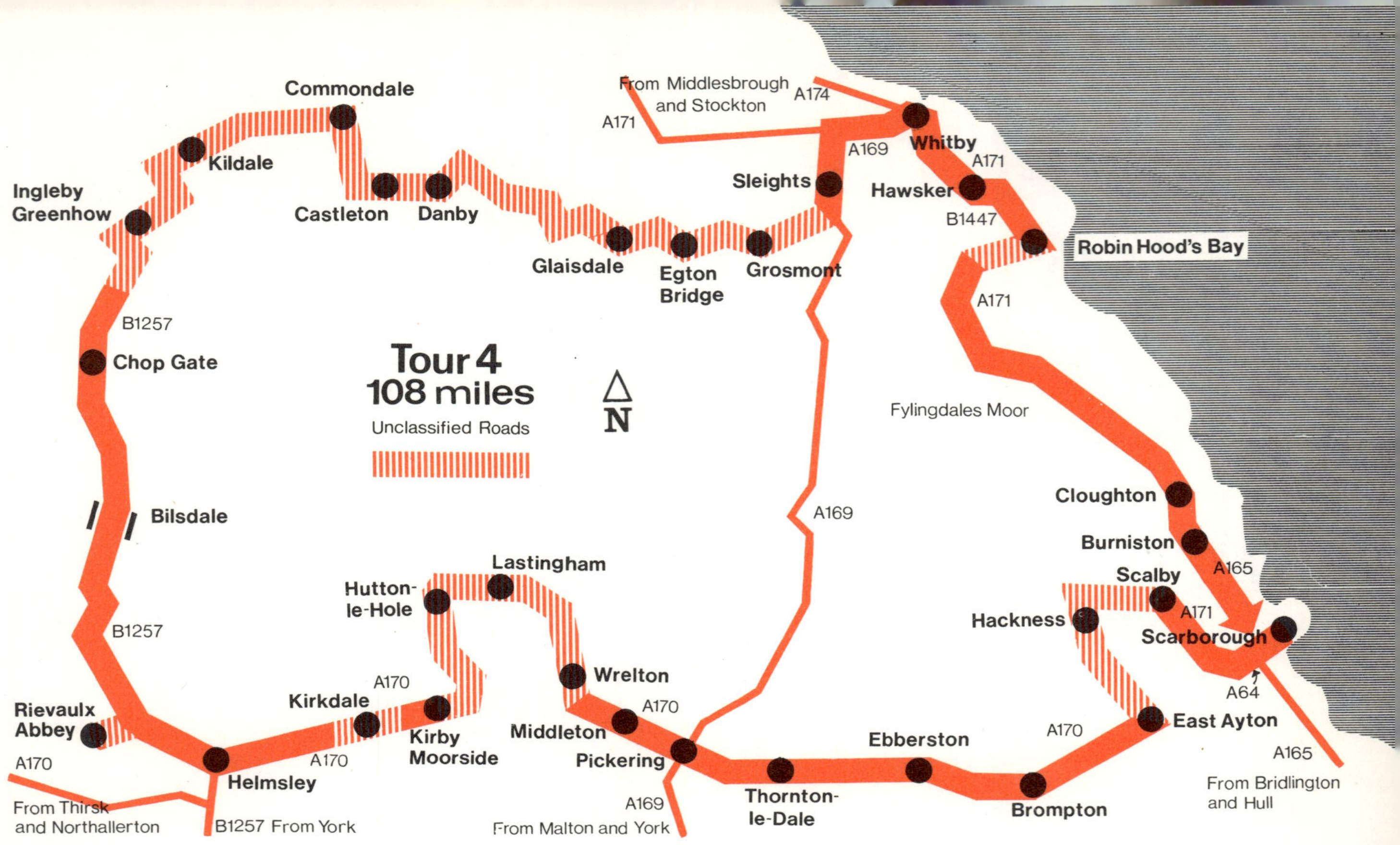
Tour 4
108 miles
Unclassified Roads
N
Commondale
Kildale
Ingleby Greenhow
Castleton
Danby
Glaisdale
Egton Bridge
Grosmont
Sleights
Whitby
Hawsker
Robin Hood's Bay
From Middlesbrough and Stockton
A174
A171
A169
A171
B1447
A171
Fylingdales Moor
Cloughton
Burniston
A165
Scalby
A171
Hackness
Scarborough
A64
East Ayton
A165
From Bridlington and Hull
A170
Brompton
Ebberston
Thornton-le-Dale
A169
Pickering
Middleton
A170
Wrelton
Lastingham
Hutton-le-Hole
Kirby Moorside
A170
Kirkdale
A170
Helmsley
B1257 From York
A169
From Malton and York
Rievaulx Abbey
A170
From Thirsk and Northallerton
B1257
Chop Gate
B1257
Bilsdale

4. The North Yorkshire Moors and Coast

This tour, starting from the favoured seaside resort of Scarborough, ascends the north side of the Vale of Pickering, a level plain about 30 miles long by 4 to 8 miles wide, bounded on the north by the dip slopes of the North Yorkshire Moors. The vale, covered in prehistoric times by a fresh-water lake, is now drained by the Rye and by the Derwent, which once escaped east into the sea, but now flows south-west through the gap between the Yorkshire Wolds and the Howardian Hills (Tour 2). The tour includes the old towns of Kirby Moorside, Pickering and Helmsley (these two with interesting castles), and makes a detour through the delightful villages of Lastingham and Hutton-le-Hole. The route passes the beautiful and extensive ruins of Rievaulx Abbey and ascends Bilsdale through the rugged Cleveland Hills (Tour 5), then descends the long and secluded Eskdale by narrow, winding and hilly roads to reach the sea at Whitby, a charming old fishing port with a grand ruined abbey. The tour, taking in the picturesque fishing village of Robin Hood's Bay, returns across the moors and high above the sea, on one of the most exciting roads in England.

Scarborough is a popular seaside resort delightfully situated on the steep shores of two fine sandy bays, separated by a high rocky headland on which stands the castle (admission 9.30 to 4, 5.30 or 7; closed Sundays until 2 in winter), which is mainly of the 12th and 13th centuries and has a barbican and a dominating keep. On the cliff edge are remains of a Roman signal station, one of a line which extended north towards Hadrian's Wall. The 12th-14th-century parish church is in the old town (much rebuilt), on the neck of the headland and above the interesting fishing harbour. The fine Marine Drive rounds the base of the headland and joins the two bays, both of which have pleasant gardens: Peasholm Park and Northstead Manor Gardens on the North Bay, the Spa with its gardens and the excellent South Cliff Gardens on the South Bay. In Vernon Road is the museum (admission weekdays, 10 to 1 and 2.30 to 5; Sundays in April-September, 2 to 5), with antiquities and ' bygones '. Oliver's Mount, a wooded hill to the south, commands a wide view.

A64 west from Scarborough station for ½ mile, then A171 (right), ascending to Scalby (2½ miles more).

Scalby, now mainly a residential suburb of Scarborough, is on a slope above the Sea Cut, a channel constructed to take the flood-waters of the Derwent into the sea at the North Bay.

Unclassified road west, climbing over to Hackness (3 miles).

Hackness is a scattered village in a beautiful wooded valley, at the junction of the Lowdales Beck with the Derwent. The interesting 12th-13th-century church contains parts of a 7th- or 8th-century cross with an inscription (uniquely) in Latin, Ogams and Runes.

Unclassified road south, down the Derwent and through the lovely Forge Valley to East Ayton (4 miles), then A170 (right) through the Vale of Pickering to Brompton (3 miles) and thence to Ebberston (3½ miles more).

Brompton has a large church, mainly of the 15th century, in which William Wordsworth was married to Mary Hutchinson in 1802, and a late-18th-century hall, the home of Sir George Cayley, a pioneer in the design of the aeroplane, who died in 1857. Ebberston has a charming small hall, built in the Palladian style in 1718 by Colen Campbell.

A170 on to Thornton-le-Dale (4 miles).

Thornton-le-Dale is an attractive village with an 18th-century hall (now a hotel) and becks running along two of its streets.

A170 on to Pickering (2½ miles).

Pickering, which gives its name to the vale, is an old market town with a restored 12th-14th-century church which has a Saxon or early-Norman font and a notable series of 15th-century wall paintings, rather too well restored in 1889. On the north chancel wall is a monument to Nicholas and Robert King, surveyors to the city of Washington. The castle (admission weekdays, 9.30 to 4, 5.30 or 7; Sundays from 2), often in Lancastrian hands, consists of two wards or baileys, the outer with a 14th-century wall strengthened by towers, the inner enclosed by a 12th-century wall rising to an early-Norman motte. Middleton (see below) has a 12th-13th-century church containing three 10th-century Saxon crosses.

A170 on through Middleton (1½ miles), then by an unclassified road (right) to Wrelton (1 mile) and on to Cropton (2 miles more), and thence left, crossing the Seven at the foot of Rosedale, to Lower Askew (1 mile) and right to Lastingham (1 mile farther).

Lastingham, a secluded village near the south edge of the North Yorkshire Moors, has a fascinating church of the late-12th and 13th centuries, originally that of a Benedictine abbey. Below the chancel is an aisled Norman crypt of about 1080, practically a lower church, containing Saxon carved stones.

Unclassified road on, at the edge of the moors, to Hutton-le-Hole (2 miles).

Hutton-le-Hole, in a wooded dale, is a charming village of stone cottages with red-pantiled roofs, scattered round a green. An old cruck-framed cottage now contains the Ryedale Folk Museum (admission daily, except Tuesdays and Fridays, in summer, 2 to 7), with old domestic utensils and agricultural implements, 'bygones' and archaeological finds.

Unclassified road down the Hutton Beck, then crossing (right) to the lower part of Farndale, the valley of the Dove, for Kirby Moorside (3 miles).

Kirby Moorside (properly Kirkby) is an attractive small stone-built town, with a broad market place round which are several old inns, notably the Black Swan, fronted by a timbered porch of 1632.

Unclassified road on to rejoin A170 in ½ mile, then by another unclassified road (right) to Kirkdale (1 mile more).

Kirkdale, at the foot of a delightful wooded dale famous for its daffodils, has a solitary small church of the 10th-13th centuries above the south doorway of which is a sundial with the longest known Saxon inscription, recording the rebuilding of the church by Orm, son of Gamal, in the days of Edward the Confessor.

Unclassified road on to rejoin A170 for Helmsley (4 miles).

Helmsley is a stone-built agricultural town on the Rye, with many fine old houses round its exceptionally broad market place. The castle (admission weekdays, 9.30 to 4, 5.30 or 7; Sundays from 2), defended by a double rampart and ditch, was mainly built by Robert de Roos in 1186-1227, the most distinctive feature being the tall keep on the east wall of the rectangular inner ward. A drive, starting to the south, leads through the beautiful grounds (admission May-August, Wednesdays, 10 to 4) of Duncombe Park, a classical house of about 1711, partly rebuilt after a fire in 1895.

B1257 west from Helmsley, climbing to the end of the lane (2½ miles) descending to Rievaulx Abbey (½ mile).

Rievaulx Abbey (admission 9.30 to 4, 5.30 or 7; closed Sunday mornings in winter), founded in 1131, stands on a shelf above the deep wooded Ryedale, and rivals Fountains as the most delightfully situated Cistercian monastery in England. The extensive and enchanting ruins include the Norman and Early English transepts of the church, the splendid choir and presbytery (of about 1230), and considerable remains of the domestic buildings, notably the chapter house, which has an ambulatory and apse (unique in an English Cistercian house). The grassy terrace above (admission weekdays, 9 to 7 or dusk; Sundays from 1), with two 18th-century classical temples, affords a lovely view of the dale and abbey.

B1257 on above Ryedale, then ascending the tributary valley of Bilsdale to Chop Gate (9½ miles).

Chop Gate is a hamlet near the head of Bilsdale, watered by the Seph, one of the long and very attractive valleys than run south from the main watershed of the Cleveland Hills (Tour 5) towards the Vale of Pickering.

B1257 on for 3 miles, through a gap in the hills, then by an unclassified road (right) to Ingleby Greenhow (2½ miles).

Ingleby Greenhow is a secluded village charmingly placed below the steep northern escarpment of the Cleveland Hills.

Unclassified road on (east) through Battersby (1½ miles), then right, under Easby Moor (see page 32) to Kildale (2 miles more) and thence across the upper waters of the Leven to Commondale

(3½ miles farther); then right, crossing the river again and the foot of Westerdale to Castleton (3½ miles).

Castleton is an old-world village among the Cleveland moorlands, near the junction of the several valleys that combine to form Eskdale, the long, quiet valley that runs east through the moorland hills to reach the sea at Whitby. No main road traverses the dale, the hamlets and farms of which are reached only by narrow, hilly and circuitous side roads.

Unclassified road on (east), branching right in ½ mile and keeping south of the Esk to Danby (1½ miles more).

Danby is a scattered moorland village which has a partly ruined castle of the Latimers and Nevilles, probably of the late-14th century, with a courtroom in which courts leet (half-yearly courts held by the lord of the manor) are still held. Duck Bridge (see below) is a late-medieval pack-horse bridge.

Unclassified road left, crossing the Esk by Duck Bridge (½ mile), then recrossing 1 mile downstream and keeping on the south side of the dale for Glaisdale (3½ miles more).

Glaisdale is a former iron-mining village at the opening of the broad dale of the same name. At the entrance to a wooded ravine on the Esk, flanked by Arncliffe Woods, is Beggar's Bridge (see below), a pack-horse bridge partly rebuilt in 1621.

Unclassified road on to Beggar's Bridge (½ mile), then right for Egton Bridge (2 miles more).

Egton Bridge, at the east end of Arncliffe Woods, has an ornate Roman Catholic church of 1867.

Unclassified road on downstream, crossing the Esk again to Grosmont (2 miles) and ascending thence to Sleights (2½ miles farther).

Sleights is a stone-built village stretched out along the steep Blue Bank, by which the moorland road from Pickering (Tour 5) descends into Eskdale, with a wide-spreading view.

A169 (left) down to Sleights Bridge (1 mile) and ascending the north side of the dale to reach A171 (1 mile more); then right by A169 to Whitby (2 miles farther).

Whitby is an entrancing old red-tiled fishing port and market town on both banks of the Esk, which reaches the sea here between steep cliffs. On the West Cliff is the modern seaside resort, less popular than Scarborough, with a fine stretch of sandy beach below. The fishermen's quarter is mainly on the east bank of the river, where Captain James Cook, who made his first voyage round the world in Whitby-built ships, served as an apprentice in 1746-9 in a house in Grape Lane. From the north end of the narrow Church Street, a flight of 199 steps climbs to St. Mary's Church, basically of the 12th century and containing an amazing array of 17th-18th-century woodwork (pulpit, galleries, box pews). A 19th-century churchyard cross commemorates the 7th-century, Old-English poet Caedmon, the 'father of English sacred song', who was a monk at Whitby Abbey. Originally founded in 657 by St. Hilda, the abbey was long the chief school of learning in the north. The beautiful ruins (admission 9.30 to 4, 5.30 or 7; closed Sunday until 2 in winter), in a dominating position on the windswept cliff nearly 200 feet above the sea, are those of a 13th-14th-century church of a foundation of about 1078 for Benedictines. The ruined Old Manor House (admission as above, but Sundays from 2 only), near by, was built in the 17th century. In Pannett Park, on the west of the town is the interesting museum and art gallery (admission weekdays, 9 or 10.30 to 1 and 2 to 4 or 5.30; closed afternoons, except Wednesday and Saturday, in winter; Sundays, 2 to 4 or 5), with a fine local history collection (ship models, etc.).

A171 south from the bridge, on the east bank of the Esk, climbing thence to Hawsker (3 miles); then B1447 (left), descending steeply to Robin Hood's Bay ($2\frac{1}{2}$ miles).

Robin Hood's Bay, near the north end of the large and beautiful bay from which it takes its name (formerly Bay Town), is an enchanting fishing village with red-tiled houses, perched irregularly on a precipitous slope above the rocky shore.

Unclassified road west, ascending (steep in places) to Fyling Thorpe ($\frac{1}{2}$ mile) and thence to Fylingdales Moor ($1\frac{1}{2}$ miles more).

Fylingdales Moor is a large tract of the heather-covered moorland between the roads from Whitby to Scarborough and to Pickering (see Tour 5, page 33).

A171 (left), across exhilarating moorland, with wide seaward views, to Cloughton ($9\frac{1}{2}$ miles) and thence to Burniston ($1\frac{1}{2}$ miles); then A165 (left), descending across the Sea Cut at Newby Mill to Scarborough ($3\frac{1}{2}$ miles more).

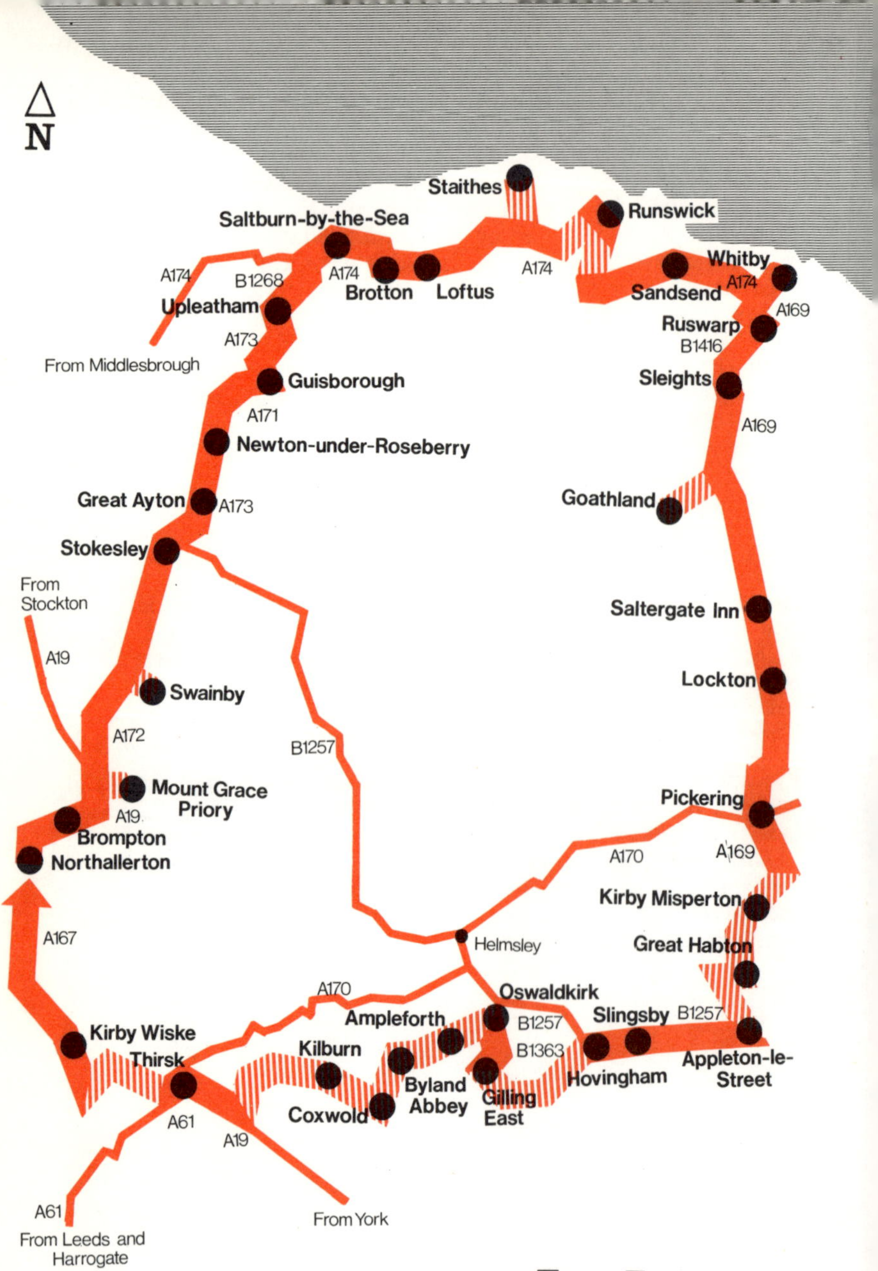

Tour 5
116 miles

Unclassified Roads

5. The Cleveland Hills and North Yorkshire Moors

This tour, like Tour 4, is confined to the North Riding of Yorkshire, and it likewise traverses the Cleveland Hills, the north-west portion of the North Yorkshire Moors, a region of heather-covered uplands with a pronounced escarpment overlooking the level plain of the Tees. To the south and east project the long ridges separating Bilsdale, Bransdale, Farndale, Rosedale and Eskdale; and to the south-west the escarpment range is prolonged by the Hambleton Hills (Tour 2). The tour takes in the old towns of Northallerton, Thirsk, Stokesley and Pickering (with a fine castle), a wealth of interesting villages, such as Great Ayton (the home of Captain Cook), Coxwold (associated with Sterne), Goathland, high on the moors, Slingsby, Hovingham, and the fishing settlements of Staithes and Runswick, as well as the seaside resort of Saltburn, the enchanting old fishing port of Whitby, and monastic houses from the priories of Mount Grace and Guisborough and the abbeys of Whitby and Byland to the modern Ampleforth Abbey.

Northallerton, in the upper part of the Vale of York, is the county town of the North Riding and a market town. The Golden Lion is the best of the 18th-century houses and inns in the broad High Street. The fine church, dominated by its 15th-century crossing tower, is in the Norman, Early English and Perpendicular styles.

A684 north-east to Brompton ($1\frac{1}{2}$ miles; on the left).

Brompton has an over-restored church containing a magnificent collection of Saxon and Viking-inspired stones, among them three well-preserved hogback tombstones and several fine crosses and shafts.

A684 on to Ellerbeck Lane End (4 miles), then A19 (left) to Mount Grace Priory (1 mile; to the right).

Mount Grace Priory (admission Tuesday-Saturday and Bank Holidays, 9 or 9.30 to 4, 6 or 7; Sundays from 2), below the wooded escarpment of the Cleveland Hills, was founded in 1398 and is the most extensive and best preserved Carthusian monastery in England. It consists of two large courts, with the church between them and the separate cells of the monks (one rebuilt in its original style) with their gardens, around the north court.

A19 on to Cleveland Tontine Inn ($\frac{1}{2}$ mile), then A172 (right) to Swainby (3 miles more; on the right).

Swainby is built along both sides of a beck, below the Cleveland escarpment.

A172 on to Stokesley (5 miles).

Stokesley is an attractive small town with many 18th-century brick houses in its wide, irregular main street.

A173 right (east) to Great Ayton (3 miles).

Great Ayton, a large village on the Leven, was the early home of Captain James Cook, who in 1736-9 attended the school, rebuilt in 1785 and now a museum. Cook's cottage, moved to Australia in 1934, has been replaced by an obelisk of Australian granite, south of the bridge. On Easby Moor (1064 feet), to the east, is a prominent monument to the circumnavigator. Roseberry Topping (1057 feet; see below), is a distinctive conical hill projecting from the main escarpment of the Cleveland Hills.

A173 on to Newton-under-Roseberry (2 miles), and for 3 miles more; then A171 (right) to Guisborough (½ mile).

Guisborough is an old market town with a wide main street, north of the Cleveland escarpment. The church has a 15th-century tower and an 18th-century nave. Guisborough Priory (admission weekdays, 9.30 to 4, 5.30 or 7; Sundays from 2) was founded for Augustinian canons by Robert de Brus between 1119 and 1124, but the chief survival is the magnificent east front of the presbytery, rebuilt after 1289.

Unclassified road north from the church, then A713 (right) for 2 miles and B1268 (left) to Upleatham (1 mile).

Upleatham, above the wooded Skelton Beck, has an old church often claimed to be the smallest in England, though it consists only of a 17th-century tower and part of the 12th-13th-century nave.

B1268 on for 2 miles, then A174 (right) for Saltburn-by-the-Sea (½ mile).

Saltburn-by-the-Sea, a quiet resort with excellent sands, was mostly laid out after 1860, on a cliff, west of the narrow ravine of the Skelton Beck.

A174 on, crossing the beck for Brotton (2 miles) and thence across the deep valley of the Kilton Beck to Loftus (2½ miles more).

Brotton and Loftus are Cleveland ironworking towns, the former with a main street made attractive by its gardens.

A174 on to Boulby (2½ miles) and thence to Staithes (1½ miles; to the left).

Staithes is a picturesque fishing village with a rock-bound harbour at the foot of a deep, narrow break in the cliffs. Boulby Cliff, rising to the west, is the highest cliff in England (over 650 feet).

A174 on for 1½ miles, then by an unclassified road (left) to Runswick (1 mile).

Runswick is a whitewashed, red-roofed fishing village on the steep side of the charming Runswick Bay, which has a good sandy beach.

Unclassified road south for 1 mile, then A174 (left), descending to Sandsend (4½ miles farther).

Sandsend is a small holiday resort, with excellent sands, at the place where two becks reach the sea after flowing through the wooded Mulgrave Castle estate.

A174 on to Whitby (3 miles), which is entered past Pannett Park.

Whitby is described in Tour 4 (pages 28-29).
A169 west (passing Pannett Park) for 1 mile, then B1416 (left), descending to Ruswarp (1 mile more).

Ruswarp is a small village and boating resort in the steep-sided valley of the Esk.
B1416 on by the river to Sleights Bridge (1½ miles), then A169 (left), ascending to Sleights (1 mile).

Sleights is described in Tour 4 (page 28).
A169 on, ascending to the North Yorkshire Moors and reaching 945 feet in 2½ miles, where an unclassified road bears right for Goathland (2 miles).

Goathland is a delightful moorland village whose farmsteads are scattered about a large open common. The surrounding valleys are noted for their slight but charming waterfalls.
A169 on over the breezy moors, with wide-spreading views, to Ellerbeck Bridge (3 miles; see below) and thence to the Saltergate Inn (2½ miles).

The Saltergate Inn has a peat fire that has burned continuously for at least 150 years. To the south-west is the Hole of Horcum, a cup-like hollow at the head of a valley that descends below the attractive villages of Levisham and Lockton (see below). On Fylingdales Moor, south-east of Ellerbeck Bridge, are the distinctive white radar domes of the Ballistic Missile Early Warning Station.
A169 on across the moors to Lockton (3 miles; to the right) and then down, east of the wooded Newton Dale, to Pickering (5 miles more).

Pickering is described in Tour 4 (page 26).
A169 on across the level Vale of Pickering for 2½ miles, then by an unclassified road (right) to Kirby Misperton (1½ miles).

Kirby Misperton has an 18th-century hall that is now the centre of the popular Flamingo Park Zoo (admission daily), with marine and other animals and a boating lake.
Unclassified road south-west to Great Habton (2½ miles), then right for 1 mile and left to Amotherby (2 miles more); then B1257 (right) to Appleton-le-Street (1 mile) and thence to Barton-le-Street (1 mile farther).

Appleton-le-Street has a 12th-14th-century church with a notable Saxon tower. Barton-le-Street has a pseudo-Norman church of 1871 incorporating rich Norman carving from the previous building.
B1257 on to Slingsby (1½ miles).

Slingsby is an attractive stone-built village with a maypole on its green and the ruins of a fine manor house of about 1643.
B1257 on to Hovingham (2 miles).

Hovingham is a delightful village enclosed by the woods of the Howardian Hills. The rebuilt church has a Saxon tower and a remarkable sculptured slab of about 800, perhaps an altar frontal. The hall was built about 1750 and has a contemporary riding school attached.

Unclassified road west through the hall grounds and over the Howardian Hills for 2½ miles, then right (north) for 1½ miles to reach B1363, then right again to Gilling East (½ mile).

Gilling East, on the north flank of the hills, has a castle (admission weekdays, 10 to 12 and 2 to 4), now a preparatory school for Ampleforth, rebuilt after 1571, incorporating a 14th-century tower, and altered in the 18th century. The Great Chamber of 1585 has a magnificent plaster ceiling, oak panelling and stained glass.

B1363 on to Oswaldkirk (2 miles), then by an unclassified road (left), passing Ampleforth Abbey (1 mile; see below) to Ampleforth (1½ miles more).

Ampleforth is on the steep southern slopes of the Hambleton Hills. The abbey, a benedictine monastery founded in 1802 in succession to the priory of Dieulouard (France), has a noted Roman Catholic college and a fine church by Sir Giles G. Scott (1919-61).

Unclassified road on below the hills to Wass (2 miles), then left to Byland Abbey (½ mile).

Byland Abbey (admission weekdays, 9.30 to 4, 5.30 or 7; Sundays from 2) has considerable remains of the church (notably the 13th-century west front) and the domestic buildings of a Cistercian monastery moved here in 1177.

Unclassified road on to Coxwold (1½ miles).

Coxwold is another delightful village with attractive stone cottages. The 15th-century church has an octagonal tower and 17th-18th-century monuments. At Shandy Hall, a 17th-century house to the west, Laurence Sterne (curate here in 1760-8) wrote part of *Tristram Shandy* and *A Sentimental Journey*.

Unclassified road on, branching right in ½ mile, to Kilburn (1½ miles more).

Kilburn is a verdant village below Roulston Scar, a scarp-face of the Hambleton Hills marked by a white horse cut in 1857. The restored Norman church has much woodwork by Robert Thompson (died 1955), whose carving ('signed' with a mouse) has enriched many Yorkshire churches and whose workshop still flourishes here.

Unclassified road west for 4½ miles via Bagby, then A19 (right) and A61 (left) to Thirsk (2½ miles).

Thirsk is described in Tour 2 (page 17).

A61 on for ¼ mile, then by an unclassified road (right) across the Vale of York for nearly 3½ miles more; then A167 (right again) via Kirby Wiske to Northallerton (6 miles).

6. From Durham to Teesdale and Weardale

This tour, starting from the fascinating old city of Durham, runs very largely through County Durham, a little-known and much maligned county, though it has many places of great interest and beauty. The route explores the lower course of the Tees, which forms the boundary with the North Riding of Yorkshire, and the middle section of Weardale, and it takes in old towns such as Stockton, Yarm, Barnard Castle and Bishop Auckland, attractive villages like Sedgefield, Norton, Hurworth, Piercebridge, Staindrop and many others, as well as the prehistoric remains at Stanwick, the medieval castles at Raby and Barnard Castle, and some interesting churches, especially the complete Saxon church at Escomb.

Durham is an historic city, the older part of which stands on a high peninsula almost encircled by the Wear. From the summit of the steep, wooded banks rise the great Norman cathedral and castle, and the view of these from the station is the finest railway view in England. Other enticing views are obtained from the riverside walks known as the Banks and from Framwelgate Bridge, of about 1400, from which the steep Silver Street ascends to the picturesque Market Place. The imposing early-medieval castle (admission weekdays during the first three weeks in April and July-September, 10 to 12.30 and 2 to 4.30; Mondays, Wednesdays and Saturdays in all other weeks, 2 to 4.30), the principal stronghold of the powerful prince-bishops of Durham, became in 1836 the nucleus of a new university (the oldest in England except for Oxford and Cambridge), which also partly occupies houses in the narrow streets on the hill top. The splendid cathedral is the finest work of Norman architecture in Britain, with the additions of a beautiful late-12th-century Galilee Chapel on the west (the burial place of the Venerable Bede, who died in 735) and the impressive 13th-century Chapel of the Nine Altars on the east. The nave, described by Dr. Johnson as of 'rocky solidity and indeterminate duration', has massive piers with remarkable incised ornament; the high roof vaults include the oldest in England, of before 1096. Among the many features of interest are Prior Castell's Clock, of about 1500, in the south transept; Bishop Cosin's fine canopied stalls, in the choir; the 14th-century bishop's throne, said to be 'the highest in Christendom'; and the delicate stone Neville screen, of about 1380. In the monk's dormitory (now the library; admission weekdays 10 to 5, Sundays 1 to 5) are Northumbrian stone crosses, etc., and remains of the wooden coffin of St. Cuthbert, brought to Durham in 995 (when the cathedral was founded) and buried behind the high altar. On Elvet Hill, south of the river, are new buildings for the university, among them the excellent Gulbenkian Museum of oriental art and archaeology (admission weekdays, 9.30 to 12 or 1 and 2.15 to 5; Sundays, 2.15 to 5 only).

Tour 6
108 miles

Unclassified Roads

A177, crossing the Wear by Elvet Bridge to New Elvet (right), then by Hallgarth Street (left) for Shincliffe (2 miles), recrossing the Wear; then on through undulating country, with collieries, to Coxhoe ($3\frac{1}{2}$ miles more) and thence to Sedgefield (5 miles farther).

Sedgefield is an attractive village with a large green and a church of the 13th and 15th centuries which contains sumptuous 17th-century woodwork.

A177 on to Thorpe Thewles ($4\frac{1}{2}$ miles) and for $1\frac{1}{2}$ miles more, then B1274 (left) to Norton (2 miles farther).

Norton, though now a suburb of Stockton, remains an unspoilt 18th-century residential village, with a tree-lined High Street. The interesting church has a Saxon crossing tower, a late-12th-century nave and transepts, and a chancel partly of the 13th century.

A19 (right) to Stockton-on-Tees ($1\frac{1}{2}$ miles).

Stockton-on-Tees is a market and industrial town that developed after the opening, in 1825, of the Stockton & Darlington Railway, the first public railway in England, and is now a port with numerous iron and steel works and other industries. In the middle of the exceptionally broad High Street are the old Town Hall of 1735 and the Market Cross of 1768. St. Thomas's, at the north end, is a classical brick church of 1712, perhaps built with the advice of Wren. Preston Hall (see below; admission weekdays, 10 to 8; Sundays 2 to 8) is now a museum of arms and armour, and natural and local history.

A19 south-west to Preston Hall ($2\frac{1}{2}$ miles), near the Tees, and thence to Egglescliffe (2 miles; on the left).

Egglescliffe, well situated on a high bank above the river, is attractively grouped round a green and the 15th-century church, which has interesting 17th-century woodwork. It overlooks Yarm, an old-world market town on level ground in a bend of the Tees, which is crossed by a bridge of about 1400 (carrying A19), and dominated by a high railway viaduct of 43 arches, built in 1849. In the wide cobbled main street are the Market Hall of 1710 and many colourful 17th-18th-century brick houses.

Unclassified road west from Egglescliffe, north of the Tees, via Aislaby, bearing left in 5 miles for Middleton St. George ($\frac{1}{2}$ mile).

Middleton St. George is a village on a high bank above the Tees, which is overlooked by the charming street of Middleton One Row.

Unclassified road on for 1 mile, then left to Neasham ($2\frac{1}{2}$ miles more) and thence (right) to Hurworth ($1\frac{1}{2}$ miles).

Neasham and Hurworth are handsome villages on the Tees, the latter with a long green and houses occupied in the 18th century by the merchants of Darlington, to the north.

Unclassified road on over the Tees to Croft (1 mile).

Croft, once a small spa, has a church whose interior is dominated by the enormous Milbanke pew, erected before 1680; the 18th-century rectory, to the west, was the boyhood home (from 1843) of 'Lewis Carroll', author of *Alice in Wonderland*.

A167 left, then by an unclassified road (right) to Middleton Tyas (5½ miles).

Middleton Tyas is a pleasant village whose church (½ mile east among the fields) is mainly of the 13th century.

Unclassified road on (west) to Scotch Corner (1 mile), on the Great North Road (A1); then A66 on again for 1½ miles more and by an unclassified road (right) to Melsonby (1½ miles).

Melsonby is another pleasant village, built along either side of a beck, with a 13th-century church which has a fine tower.

Unclassified road left (west) for 1½ miles, then right for Forcett (2 miles more), then right again to Stanwick (1 mile).

Stanwick is a scattered hamlet enclosed by the extensive earthworks of Stanwick Camp, a large fortified settlement of the Brigantes, constructed about A.D. 50. Here the tribe, under their chief, Venutias, made a final effort in A.D. 71 to stem the Roman advance.

Unclassified road on to Aldbrough (1½ miles), then left (north-east) for 1 mile; then B6275 (left again) to cross the Tees for Piercebridge (2 miles farther).

Piercebridge, built (unusually) on the exact site of a Roman fort (on the road from York to Corbridge), is a village of low white-washed and red-tiled cottages spaced round a tree-shaded green.

A67 (left) to Gainford (2½ miles).

Gainford, a village charmingly situated on the north bank of the Tees, has an almost complete, if restored, 13th-century church.

A67 on to Winston (2 miles) and thence to Barnard Castle (6½ miles more).

Barnard Castle is a delightful old market town with broad streets and many 18th-century stone houses, in a beautiful position on the steep north bank of the Tees. Charles Dickens stayed at the King's Head Hotel in the Market Place, while investigating conditions in the Yorkshire schools (described in *Nicholas Nickleby*). Below the octagonal 18th-century Market House is Blagroves House, a 16th-century town mansion. The castle (admission 9.30 to 4, 5.30 or 7; Sundays from 2), built by the Baliols after 1093, was confiscated in 1296 after the revolt of John Baliol, King of Scotland. The Bowes Museum (admission weekdays, 10 to 4, 5 or 5.30; Sundays, 2 to 4 or 5, east of the town, is a grandiose late-19th-century mansion in the style of a French château, built for John Bowes and his French wife, and now containing period rooms with outstanding collections of porcelain, furniture, paintings and ecclesiastical art.

A67 back for 1 mile, then A688 (left) to Staindrop (5 miles more).

Staindrop is an attractive village with a long tree-shaded green. The interesting church shows work from the Saxon period to the 15th century and contains splendid 15th-century and later monuments of the Nevilles (see below).

A688 on past Raby Castle (1 mile).

Raby Castle (admission Easter and May-September, Wednesdays, week-ends and Bank Holidays, 2 to 5; daily, except Fridays, August to first week in September), the seat of the Nevilles and since 1626 of the Vanes, is one of the largest and most magnificent 14th-century castles in England, partly remodelled in the mid-19th-century and containing many fine English and other paintings.

A688 on to West Auckland (4 miles) and thence north-east for 2 miles more, then A6073 (right) to St. Andrew Auckland (1 mile).

West Auckland is a characteristic village with 17th-century houses round a large green, on the edge of the Durham coalfield. St. Andrew Auckland has a large 13th-century church containing a Northumbrian cross of about 800 with fine carving.

A6072 (left) and A688 (right) to Bishop Auckland (1½ miles).

Bishop Auckland is a market and industrial town on the Wear. Auckland Castle, a seat of the Bishops of Durham since the 12th century is mainly of the 16th and 18th centuries, but the beautiful chapel was converted from a hall by Bishop Cosin, who was buried here in 1672. In the wooded Bishop's Park, reached through a Gothick gatehouse of 1760, is an unusual 18th-century deer house.

A689 west from the market place, then B6284 (left) to join A6073, from which (in 1½ miles) a side road descends to Escomb (1 mile more).

Escomb, on the Wear, has a complete Saxon church, probably of the 7th century and certainly one of the earliest in England, judiciously restored, with new furnishings, by Sir Albert Richardson.

A6073 on (west) to High Etherley (1½ miles), then A68 (right) to Witton-le-Wear (3 miles more).

Witton-le-Wear is a village attractively situated above the north bank of the river, with a medieval tower-house remodelled in the 17th century. Witton Castle, in a fine park (admission daily in summer) on the south side of the Wear, is a 15th-century tower-house extended and altered in the 18th and 19th centuries.

A68 on, ascending to Tow Law (6 miles; see Tour 7) and thence for 1½ miles, reaching over 1,000 feet; then B6296 (right), descending to Lanchester.

Lanchester, a market village in the Browney Valley, has a fine church, chiefly of the 12th and 13th centuries, with Roman columns in the north arcade and a Roman altar in the porch.

A691 east down the valley to Witton Gilbert (4½ miles) and on for 2 miles more, then over the Great North Road (A1) to enter Durham (2 miles farther) by North Road.

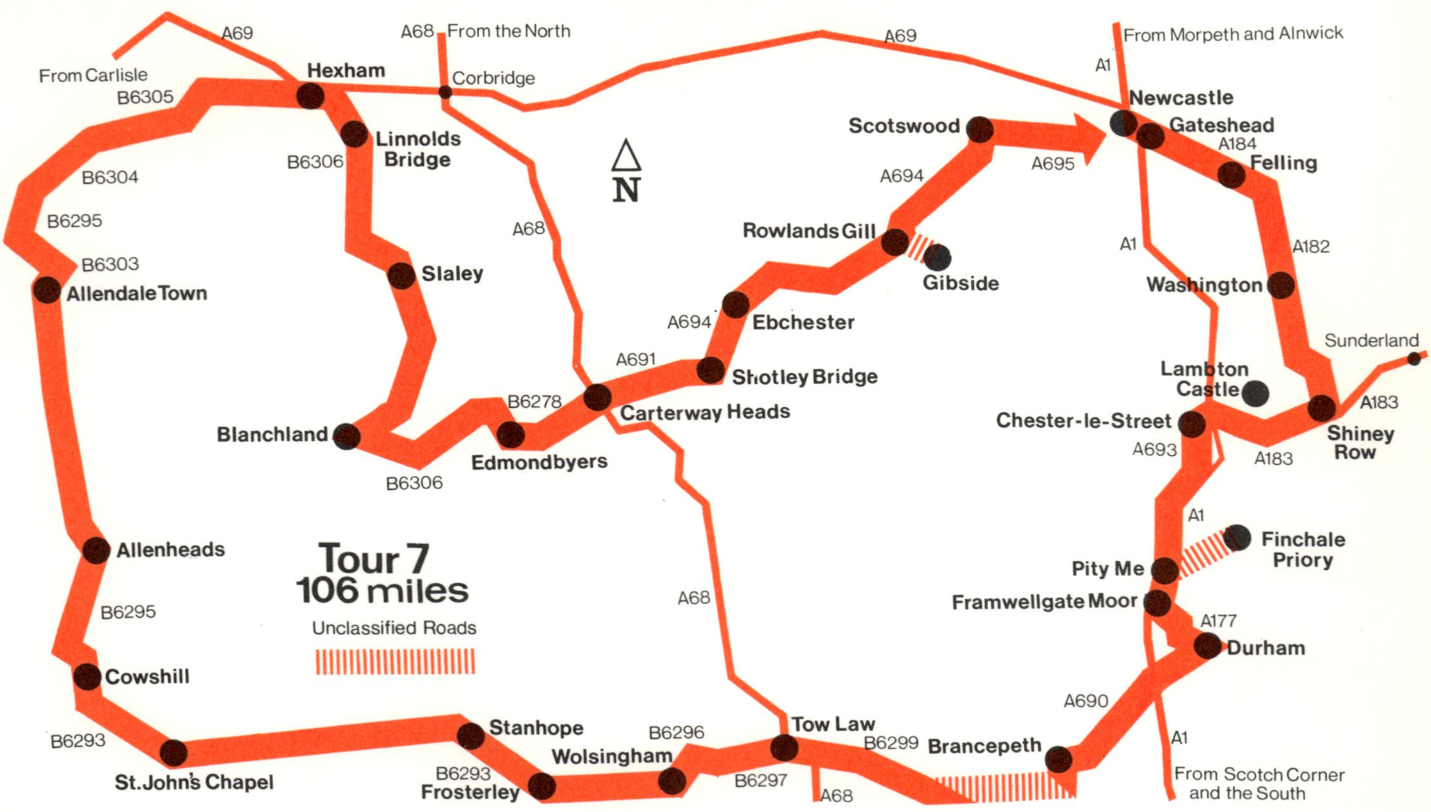

Tour 7
106 miles
Unclassified Roads
N
From Carlisle
A69
Hexham
A68
From the North
Corbridge
From Morpeth and Alnwick
A1
Newcastle
Gateshead
A184
Felling
Scotswood
A695
A694
Rowlands Gill
Gibside
A182
Washington
Ebchester
Shotley Bridge
A691
Carterway Heads
B6278
Edmondbyers
B6306
Blanchland
Slaley
Linnolds Bridge
B6305
B6304
B6295
B6303
Allendale Town
Allenheads
Cowshill
B6293
St. John's Chapel
Stanhope
Frosterley
Wolsingham
B6296
B6297
Tow Law
B6299
Brancepeth
A690
Durham
A177
Framwellgate Moor
Pity Me
Finchale Priory
Chester-le-Street
A693
A183
Shiney Row
Lambton Castle
Sunderland
From Scotch Corner and the South

7. Weardale, Allendale and the Derwent Valley

This tour, like Tour 6, explores County Durham, but it also takes in that part of Northumberland south of the Tyne. Starting from Newcastle upon Tyne, a busy industrial city with many places of historic interest, the route first goes through a colliery district via Washington, which contains the partly-medieval house of the Washington family, and then through the old town of Chester-le-Street, near the impressive Lumley Castle. From the enchanting cathedral city of Durham it traverses the long Weardale almost to its head, then crosses the moors to descend the beautifully wooded Allendale and goes on to Hexham, a market town on the Tyne which has a priory church that is full of interest. The tour crosses the moors again to the fascinating village of Blanchland, then descends the richly wooded valley of the Derwent, the boundary between Northumberland and Durham, to cross the Tyne above Newcastle.

From Newcastle by A1 via Pilgrim Street and across the Tyne Bridge to Gateshead (½ mile), an industrial town on the south bank, then by A184 (left) to Felling (2 miles more) and on for 1½ miles; then A182 (right) via Great Usworth to Washington (3 miles farther).

Washington is a colliery town that has an old village as its nucleus and has become the centre of a New Town, designated in 1964. The 17th-century Old Hall (admission daily, except Friday, 10 to 1 and 2 to 6 or dusk) incorporates parts of an early-medieval house, the home from 1183 to 1613 of the Washington family and their lineal descendants. The conspicuous Penshaw Monument of 1844, on a hill beyond the Wear, commemorates the 1st Earl of Durham, Governor-General of Canada.

A182 on, crossing the Wear to New Penshaw (2½ miles) and thence to Shiney Row (½ mile), then A183 (right), skirting the wooded grounds of Lambton Castle (2 miles).

Lambton Castle, a 19th-century mansion, formerly the seat of the Earls of Durham, is now a residential college for adult education.

A183 on, recrossing the Wear, for 1½ miles, then A1 (left) and A693 (right) to Chester-le-Street (1 mile).

Chester-le-Street is a market and colliery town west of the Wear. The monks of Lindisfarne (see Holy Island, page 54), bringing the body of St. Cuthbert, settled here in 883, after eight years of wandering, and here it remained until the see was transferred in 995 to Durham. The 13th-14th-century church has a slender tower and spire, 169 feet high, with an anchorite's cell attached. In the north aisle are 14 effigies of the Lumley family, all but three made for John Lord Lumley after 1594. Lumley Castle, to the east beyond the river, is a characteristically late-14th-century castle, now a hall of residence for Durham University.

A693 on for 1 mile, then A1 (right) to Pity Me ($2\frac{1}{2}$ miles more), a hamlet from which unclassified roads lead east and north-east to Finchale Priory ($2\frac{1}{2}$ miles).

Finchale Priory (admission weekdays 9.30 to 4, 5.30 or 7; Sundays from 2), delightfully placed on the bank of the rocky Wear, was founded in 1196 for Benedictines. The remains, chiefly of the 13th and 14th centuries, consist of the church, the domestic buildings (including the fine refectory) and the prior's house.

A1 on from Pity Me to Framwellgate Moor (1 mile), then A177 (left) to Durham ($1\frac{1}{2}$ miles more), by North Road and Silver Street.

Durham is described in Tour 6 (page 35).

A690 south-west, leaving Durham by Silver Street and Crossgate (left) and crossing A1 at Neville's Cross (1 mile).

Neville's Cross, on the Great North Road, has the remains of a cross commemorating a battle of 1346 in which the Scots were defeated by the English and David II taken prisoner.

A690 on over the Wear for Brancepeth ($3\frac{1}{2}$ miles).

Brancepeth has an imposing castle (admission to grounds), the seat before 1569 of the powerful house of Neville, Earls of Westmorland, but partly rebuilt in the 19th century. The near-by 13th-15th-century church is remarkable for its 14th-16th-century monuments of the Nevilles and its sumptuous woodwork introduced by John Cosin, rector here from 1625, and later Bishop of Durham.

A690 on for $\frac{1}{2}$ mile, then by an unclassified road (right) for $2\frac{1}{2}$ miles more; then B6299 (right again) for a further 3 miles, reaching nearly 1000 feet, and A68 on to Tow Law ($\frac{1}{2}$ mile).

Tow Law is a high-lying market town, with iron foundries, and commands a wide view over the Pennine moorlands to the west.

B6297 on for 2 miles, then B6296 (left) to Wolsingham ($1\frac{1}{2}$ miles).

Wolsingham is a small town with 16th-18th-century houses, at the entrance to the narrow upper part of Weardale.

B6293 (right) through the valley to Frosterley ($3\frac{1}{2}$ miles).

Frosterley is a village long noted for its marble, a black limestone rich in fossils and used in many church fonts.

B6293 on to Stanhope ($2\frac{1}{2}$ miles).

Stanhope, an old town with a 13th-century church, is the capital of upper Weardale and the centre of a quarrying district with cement works and lead mines. Near the Heathery Burn, to the east, is a limestone cave in which the tools of Bronze Age metal workers were discovered.

B6293 on up Weardale to St. John's Chapel (7 miles).

St. John's Chapel is an attractive village engaged in agriculture and quarrying and situated in the pastoral upper section of the dale.

B6293 on, following the Wear, to Cowshill (3 miles).

Cowshill is a hamlet near the head of Weardale from which B6293 goes on to Killhope Cross, the highest point reached by any main road in England (2056 feet). The road, climbing over to Allenheads (see below) and reaching over 1850 feet at the point where it leaves County Durham for Northumberland, likewise affords extensive views over the swelling moorlands which stretch south-west towards Cross Fell.

B6295 (right) from Cowshill, crossing to Allenheads (3 miles).

Allenheads is a secluded village charmingly enclosed by trees near the head of East Allendale. Another high-level road, ascending to 1760 feet, crosses the moorlands east towards Rookhope and Stanhope.

B6295 on, down the long East Allendale, to Allendale Town (7½ miles).

Allendale Town is a small agricultural town and summer resort above the beautiful pastoral and wooded dale of the East Allen, which is surrounded by high moorlands.

B6303 (right) for 1½ miles, then B6295 again (right) for 2 miles more, ascending over Emertley Hill (1034 feet); then B6304 right for 1 mile and B6305 (right again), crossing a moorland with a fine view over South Tynedale towards Hadrian's Wall before descending to join A69 in Hexham (6 miles farther).

Hexham, on the south bank of the Tyne, is a delightful agricultural town with a long main street. To the east of the Market Place is the 14th-century Moot Hall (now a library; admission Monday and Wednesday, 6 to 8; Wednesdays also 2.30 to 4.30), once the tower-house of the bailiff of the Archbishop of York, who was lord of the regality of Hexham. Farther east is the Manor Office of 1332, the medieval prison of the regality, the only one in England. The cathedral-like Priory Church, west of the Market Place, retains the original crypt of the 7th-century church built by St. Wilfrid. The Norman nave, destroyed by the Scots in 1296, was rebuilt in 1908, but the magnificent choir and the transepts, with their unique and well-worn night stairs leading from the canons' dormitory, are mainly of the 12th and 13th centuries. In the south transept are a Roman monument and a Saxon cross of the 8th century. The choir is full of interesting features, including a Saxon bishop's stone chair, 15th-century chantry chapels, and numerous paintings on the rood-screen and elsewhere. The Roman town of *Corstopitum* (Tour 8, page 47), 3 miles east, may be reached by A6079, crossing the river by an 18th-century bridge, and thence by an unclassified road to the right.

B6306 south from Hexham, climbing steeply through well-wooded country before descending to Linnolds Bridge ($2\frac{1}{2}$ miles).

Linnolds Bridge crosses the beautiful Devil's Water, which lower down flows through the wooded gorge of Swallowship towards Dilston. Above the bridge are the Hexham Levels, or the Linnolds, the site of the Battle of Hexham (1464) in which the Lancastrians under Henry VI were roundly defeated by the Yorkists under John Neville, later Earl of Northumberland, and the king was forced to flee.

B6306 on, ascending again to Slaley (3 miles), then running at the edge of the moors before dropping down to Blanchland (5 miles more).

Blanchland is an enchanting village in the sequestered upper valley of the Derwent. Remains of a 12th-century abbey are preserved in the church and built into the planned village, whose unusual square is entered through the abbey gateway, of about 1500. The charming stone houses were built soon after 1752, when also the Lord Crewe Arms Inn was formed out of 13th-century ruins, probably those of the abbey guest house.

B6306 on, crossing the Derwent and re-entering County Durham, for Edmondbyers ($4\frac{1}{2}$ miles).

Edmondbyers is a characteristic moorside village built round a large green above the Derwent Valley.

B6278 (left), recrossing the river to Carterway Heads ($2\frac{1}{2}$ miles), then A691 on, descending to Shotley Bridge (3 miles farther).

Shotley Bridge is a village on the Durham side of the Derwent, in the attractively wooded valley. On the hill above to the south-east are the huge iron and steel works at Consett, a dramatic background when the great furnaces light the sky at night.

A694 (left) down the Derwent to Ebchester ($1\frac{1}{2}$ miles).

Ebchester has a church, mostly rebuilt, on the site of the Roman fort of *Vindomora,* and under the tower is a Roman altar. Robert Surtees, the creator of 'Jorrocks', was buried (in 1864) in the churchyard.

A694 on through the wooded valley to Rowlands Gill (5 miles).

Rowlands Gill is a village on the north bank of the Derwent. In the fine grounds of Gibside, a dismantled mansion of the 17th century and later, on the other side, of the river, is a charming classical chapel (admission Good Friday to September, daily, except Tuesdays, 2 to 6; October to before Easter, Wednesdays, Saturdays and Sundays, 2 to 6 or dusk), begun in 1760 by James Paine. It is connected by an avenue with a prominent Column of Liberty, 140 feet high, built in 1757.

A694 on down the Derwent Valley for 4 miles, then A695 (right) over the Tyne by Scotswood Bridge, rebuilt in 1968, and on to Newcastle (3 miles more), by Scotswood Road.

8. Tynedale and Hadrian's Wall

This tour, wholly in Northumberland, ascends the Tyne from Newcastle as far as Corbridge, a charming village near the extensive remains of a large Roman garrison town. It then ascends to follow the most fascinating section of the great wall of Hadrian, which is not only of supreme antiquarian interest, but traverses much wild and exhilarating country, crossing the lovely North Tynedale at Chollerford. From Greenhead the route returns through the quietly charming South Tynedale to Hexham, a delightful market town with a beautiful priory church. From here, the tour ascends North Tynedale as far as the old town of Bellingham, then crosses the moors to reach the finest of the roads to Scotland (see Tour 10) at Otterburn. Thence it returns to Newcastle over the moors again and by way of the graceful mansion of Wallington.

Hadrian's Wall, stretching right across country from Wallsend, on the Tyne, to Bowness-on-Solway, a distance of over 73 miles, is a great fortification built in A.D. 122-30, under the orders of the Emperor Hadrian, as the frontier of the Roman province of Britain. The wall itself, built of stone, stood originally about 15 feet high and varies from 7½ to 9 feet thick. On its north side, for most of its course, it is followed by a ditch about 27 feet wide, and to the south, at a short but varying distance, is the Vallum, a flat-bottomed ditch 20 feet wide at the top, running between earth mounds and intended to protect the fortification on that side. The wall was patrolled from so-called 'milecastles', small barrack buildings about 1,620 yards apart, and between each of these were two smaller turrets at equal spaces. The Roman garrison was quartered in 17 large forts of rectangular shape, some of which were built slightly later than the wall and replaced an earlier series of forts along the Stanegate, a road farther south, parallel to the Tyne. The finest remaining sections of the wall are near Chollerford and between Sewingshields and Birdoswald (in Cumberland, west of Greenhead); the most interesting forts are those at Chesters (near Chollerford) and Housesteads. From Newcastle to Sewingshields the remains of the wall were used as a foundation for the Military Road to Carlisle, built after the Jacobite rising of 1745 (when the Hanoverian troops were unable to get across country and come to grips with Prince Charles Edward Stuart), and in consequence there is little of the wall itself to be seen. The ditch and vallum, however, are distinctive for most of their course beyond the suburbs of Newcastle.

From Newcastle upon Tyne by Westgate Road and A69 to Benwell (2 miles) and thence to Heddon-on-the-Wall (5½ miles).

Benwell is a residential suburb of Newcastle, and in an estate here are the remains of a small temple that stood outside the Roman fort of *Condercum*. At Heddon practically the first upstanding

Tour 8
120 miles

lengths of the wall can be seen, and the village has an interesting church of the 12th and 13th centuries.

A69 on for 1½ miles, then by an unclassified road (left) descending to Wylam (1 mile); then beside the Tyne to Ovingham (2 miles more).

Ovingham has a 13th-century church with a Saxon tower, near the foot of which is the grave of Thomas Bewick, the famous engraver. Prudhoe, on the steep opposite bank of the river, has a castle of the 12th-14th centuries.

Unclassified road on to Bywell (2½ miles).

Bywell, attractively situated on the river, is a 'decayed' village with a 15th-century gatehouse-tower and two churches in adjacent churchyards, both mainly of the 13th century, though one has a fine Saxon tower.

Unclassified road on for 3 miles, then A69 (left) to Corbridge (1½ miles).

Corbridge, a large and interesting village on the north bank of the stony Tyne, was once the capital of the Saxon Northumbria. The church, mostly of the 13th century, has a unique Saxon porch-tower with a Roman arch, and at the edge of the churchyard is a 14th-century fortified vicarage of a type peculiar to Northumberland. To the west, north of the river, are the considerable remains of *Corstopitum* (admission daily, 9.30 to 4, 5.30 or 7; Sundays in winter from 2), an important garrison town and a supply-depot serving the legions on Hadrian's Wall. The excavated buildings include a huge storehouse, one of the largest Roman buildings discovered in Britain; and the museum contains a fine collection of inscribed and sculptured stones.

A68 right (north), ascending to Stagshawbank (3 miles).

Stagshawbank, an open common long famous for the large sheep fair held here, is at the point where Hadrian's Wall was penetrated by Dere Street, the Roman road that led from *Corstopitum* into Scotland. At Halton Chesters, ½ mile east on B6318, are the extensive earthworks of the fort of *Onnum*, and at Halton, ½ mile farther south, is a 14th-century pele-tower of typical Border type.

B6318 left (west), following the line of the wall, to St. Oswald's (3 miles) and thence down to Low Brunton (1 mile).

St. Oswald's is a solitary 18th-century chapel in a lonely position just north of the wall, marking the place where St. Oswald, King of Northumbria, pitched his camp before the great battle of A.D. 634 in which he defeated the heathen King Cadwalla. At Low Brunton the road up North Tynedale (page 49) cuts through the line of Hadrian's Wall. To the south is a fine stretch of the wall, with an excellent example of a turret.

B6318 on over the North Tyne to Chollerford (½ mile) and thence to Chesters (½ mile), on the left.

Chollerford is in a delightful pastoral and wooded valley, and here the river is crossed by a late-18th-century bridge. Chesters has a fine park containing the extensive remains of the Roman cavalry fort of *Cilurnum* (admission weekdays, 9 or 9.30 to 4, 5 or 5.30; Sundays, 2 to 4, 4.30 or 5), which stood on the wall. Near the west bank of the North Tyne is the large and well-preserved bath-house, the finest in Britain. When the river is low, two piers of a Roman bridge are revealed, and on the farther bank is part of the east abutment. The museum in the park contains an outstanding collection of antiquities from the wall.

B6318, ascending out of the valley to Limestone Corner (3 miles) and going on thence to Carrawburgh (1½ miles).

Limestone Corner (823 feet), where the Vallum and ditch are cut through the solid rock, affords a wide view over North Tynedale to the Simonside and Cheviot Hills. Beyond the farm of Carrawburgh are the earthworks of the fort of *Brocolitia,* and outside these are the remarkable remains of a Temple of Mithras, of the 3rd century, excavated since 1950.

B6318 on towards Sewingshields (2 miles).

Sewingshields is a farm to the right of the Military Road, which, like the Vallum, diverges south from the line of Hadrian's Wall. The wall itself climbs along the crest of the Great Whin Sill, a long escarpment of basaltic crags, commanding a wild view over the Northumbrian moors to the Border hills.

B6318 on, passing south of Housesteads (in 2½ miles), and thence to the Twice Brewed Inn (2½ miles more).

Housesteads, nearly ½ mile north of the road by a footpath, stands on the edge of the Whin Sill. The well-preserved remains of the infantry fort of *Vercovicium* (admission daily, 9.30 to 4, 5.30 or 7; closed Sundays until 2 in winter) are the most interesting and the finest in situation of all the forts on the wall. A museum near the farm here contains models and plans, as well as finds made in the neighbourhood. Beyond the wall are the Northumberland Lakes, in a moorland setting of extreme desolation. To the west of Housesteads is a fine example of a milecastle, and it is worth following the wall, on foot, over Hotbank Crags to the sheer rock face above the charmingly situated Crag Lough, a distance of about 1½ miles. The Twice Brewed Inn is in a very solitary position on the Military Road. To the north-west rises Winshields Crag (1230 feet), part of the Great Whin Sill, where Hadrian's Wall reaches its greatest height. The far-reaching view in clear weather includes the Scottish hills to the north and north-west, Cross Fell on the Pennines to the south, and Saddleback and Skiddaw, in the Lake District, to the south-west. To the west, the wall is less well preserved, though a good section can be seen, where it traverses the line of basalt crags known as the Nine Nicks of Thirlwall.

B6318 on from the inn to Greenhead (6 miles).

Greenhead is on the Tipalt Burn, a tributary of the South Tyne, at the junction of the Military Road with the main Newcastle-Carlisle road. For the continuation of Hadrian's Wall to Gilsland and beyond, see Letts Motor Tour Guide to *The Lake District, the Pennines and Yorkshire Dales*.

A69 left (east), entering South Tynedale before reaching Haltwhistle (3½ miles).

Haltwhistle is a pleasant market town with a complete 13th-century church. Beyond the river, to the south-west, is Bellister Castle, a 17th-century house attached to a ruined, late-medieval pele-tower.

A69 on through the dale to Bardon Mill (4½ miles) and thence to Haydon Bridge (4 miles).

Bardon Mill is a village on the north bank of the South Tyne. From the main road, 1½ miles farther on, a bridge crosses the river to the 19th-century Ridley Hall. To the east of this are the beautiful Allen Banks, with woods and crags bordering the dale of the Allen. Haydon Bridge is a small town on both banks of the South Tyne, which is crossed by a long bridge.

A69 on south of the river, with charming views, to Hexham (7 miles).

Hexham is described in Tour 7 (page 43).

A69 on and A6079 (left), crossing the Tyne, then ascending the east side of North Tynedale to Wall (4 miles).

Wall is a village attractively spaced round a large green on the slopes of the broad dale, south of the line of Hadrian's Wall.

A6079 on to Low Brunton (1 mile; see page 47) and thence on to Chollerton (1½ miles more).

Chollerton has a church with a south arcade of about 1150 built of Roman monolithic columns, probably from Chesters, and a Roman altar converted into a font. Beside the churchyard is a rare church stable, perhaps of the 18th century.

Unclassified road (left) up the dale to Barrasford (1½ miles) and thence to Chipchase Castle (3 miles more).

Barrasford faces across the Tyne to Haughton Castle, which is partly of the 13th and 14th centuries. Chipchase Castle is a 17th-18th-century mansion, built on to a 14th-century pele-tower, and in the fine park is a chapel of about 1740 with its original fittings.

Unclassified road on to Wark-on-Tyne (1½ miles).

Wark-on-Tyne, in a richly wooded section of the dale, was once the capital of the regality of Tynedale, and to the south is the motte-hill of its castle.

B6320 right (north) to Bellingham (5 miles).

Bellingham is an old town in an open part of North Tynedale, with a church which has a 13th-century chancel and a nave remodelled in the 17th century, when the unusual ribbed-stone barrel vault was provided. An unclassified road penetrates the upper reach of the dale, entering the Border Forest Park, a tract of lonely country consisting partly of open, barren moorland but including the largest man-made forest in Britain. The forest park, established in 1955, is about 280 square miles in extent, and some five-eighths of this are under plantation. The road ascends to Lewisburn (14½ miles), where there is a museum (admission Easter-September, Saturdays and Sundays, 2 to 5; daily during the last week in July and the first in August) illustrating the varied wild life of the forest, and thence to Kielder (2½ miles), a village built in 1952 by the Forestry Commission near the 18th-century Kielder Castle, formerly shooting-lodge of the Duke of Northumberland, 3 miles beyond which the road enters Scotland to descend Liddesdale (see Letts Motor Tour Guide to *The Scottish Lowlands and the Borders*).

B6320 on (north), ascending over the moors, with wide views, to Hareshaw Head (4 miles; 1019 feet), descending thence across the Roman Dere Street (A68; 2½ miles) and the Rede to Otterburn (1½ miles).

Otterburn is described in Tour 10 (page 60).

A696 (right), crossing the Elsdon Burn and winding up over Ottercops Moss (1083 feet), and descending to Kirkwhelpington (9 miles); then by an unclassified road (left) for 2½ miles, and B6342 (right) to Wallington (½ mile).

Wallington (admission April-September, Mondays, Wednesdays, Thursdays, Saturdays, Sundays and Good Friday, 2 to 6) is a charming house of the 17th and 18th centuries with good plaster-work by Italian craftsmen and exquisite porcelain and furniture. The central hall, added after 1846, is decorated with scenes from Northumbrian history by William Bell Scott, Ruskin and others. The delightful grounds were perhaps laid out by Lancelot 'Capability' Brown, the great 18th-century landscape gardener, who was born in 1716 at Kirkharle (a hamlet 1½ miles south-west).

B6342 on for 1 mile, crossing the Wansbeck by a graceful 18th-century bridge, then by an unclassified road (left) for 1 mile more; then A696 (left again) to Belsay (4½ miles).

Belsay is a small model village of about 1840, at the gates of Belsay Hall (1810-17), in the grounds of which is the 'Castle', a 14th-century pele-tower with 17th-18th-century additions.

A696 on to Ponteland (5½ miles).

Ponteland is a growing residential village with an interesting 12th-14th-century church, and a medieval tower-house in the garden of the 18th-century Old Rectory.

A696 on to Newcastle (7½ miles), which is entered by Barrack Road and Gallowgate.

9. The Northumberland Coast

This tour, starting from Morpeth (now being by-passed by the Great North Road), explores the coastal region of Northumberland, the northernmost county of England and one of the most beautiful, as well as being one of the least spoilt and most sparsely inhabited (outside the relatively small colliery and industrial area). Off the coast, which is notable for its long stretches of firm sand, are the historic Farne Islands and Holy Island, the birthplace of Christianity in the North of England. The tour takes in several splendid Border castles, such as Warkworth, Dunstanburgh, Bamburgh and Norham, beautiful gardens like those of Howick and Cragside, the well-preserved Brinkburn Priory, market towns such as Morpeth, Rothbury, Wooler, at the foot of the Cheviot Hills (Tour 10), and Berwick-upon-Tweed, with its unique Elizabethan fortifications; old fishing villages and quiet seaside resorts like Alnmouth, Craster and Seahouses (the port for the Farne Islands); and a wealth of charming villages.

Morpeth is a market town in the attractively wooded valley of the Wansbeck. Facing the market place are the rare 15th-century Curfew Tower and the Town Hall, built in 1714 by Vanbrugh. To the south of the river are the motte and 14th-century gatehouse of the castle; and farther south is the good 14th-century church.

A197 east, on the north side of the Wansbeck, to Pegswood (2½ miles), then by an unclassified road (right) to Bothal (1½ miles).

Bothal is a small model village beautifully situated on the Wansbeck. The ruined castle is entered through a bold, 14th-century gatehouse-tower; the 13th-14th-century church has a bell-cote of the Northumbrian pattern, probably of the 13th century.

Unclassified road on for 1½ miles to rejoin A197, then A1068 (left), avoiding the colliery town of Ashington, to Widdrington (6 miles more), a village lying inland from the secluded Druridge Bay, and on for 5 miles farther; then by an unclassified road (left) before reaching Amble, a coal-exporting town at the mouth of the Coquet, to rejoin A1068 at the entrance to Warkworth (2 miles).

Warkworth is enchantingly situated on a narrow peninsula almost encircled by the Coquet, which runs below red sandstone cliffs in a deep-set dale. The neck of the peninsula is defended by the castle (admission daily, 9.30 to 4, 5.30 or 7; closed Sunday mornings in winter), the magnificent stronghold of the Percy family since 1332. Scenes in Shakespeare's *Henry IV* are set here. The considerable remains, mainly of the 13th century, include the gatehouse, on the south wall, the Carrickfergus and other curtain towers, and the great hall, with the Lion Tower added about 1480. On a motte to the north rises the large and intricately designed 15th-century keep. The main street descends steeply from the castle to the market place and the fortified 14th-century bridge, near which is the church,

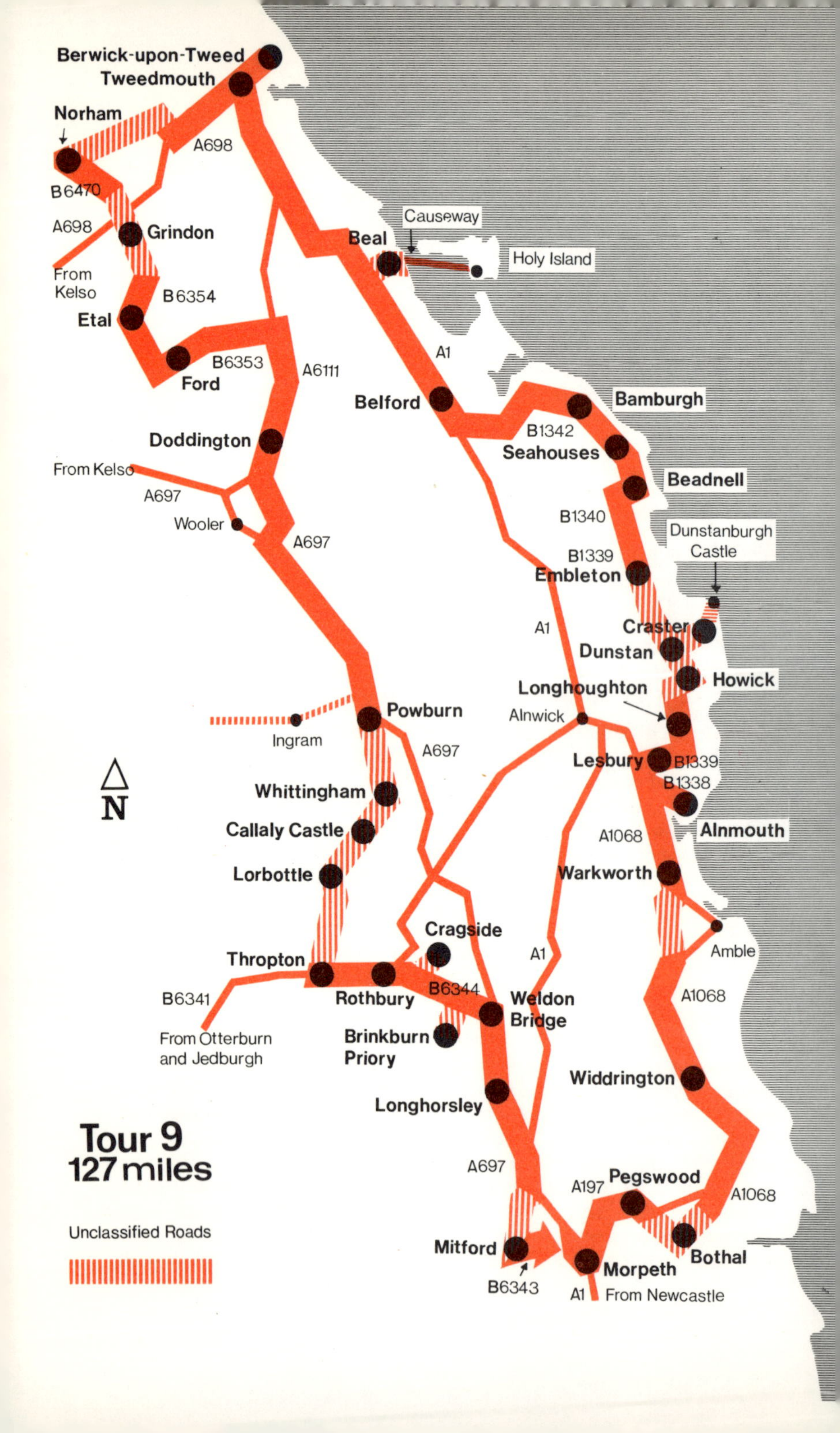
Berwick-upon-Tweed
Tweedmouth
Norham
A698
B6470
A698
Grindon
From Kelso
B6354
Etal
Ford
B6353
A6111
Causeway
Holy Island
Beal
A1
Belford
Bamburgh
B1342
Seahouses
Beadnell
Doddington
From Kelso
A697
Wooler
A697
B1340
B1339
Embleton
Dunstanburgh Castle
A1
Craster
Dunstan
Howick
Longhoughton
Alnwick
Powburn
Ingram
A697
Lesbury
B1339
B1338
Alnmouth
Whittingham
Callaly Castle
Lorbottle
A1068
Warkworth
Amble
Cragside
A1
Thropton
Rothbury
B6344
Weldon Bridge
B6341
From Otterburn and Jedburgh
Brinkburn Priory
A1068
Widdrington
Longhorsley
A697
A197
Pegswood
A1068
Mitford
Bothal
Morpeth
B6343
A1
From Newcastle
N
Tour 9
127 miles
Unclassified Roads

partly Norman and of the 14th century, but with an unusual vaulted chancel of about 1130 and a tower of about 1200. Hewn out of the rock on the north bank of the river, and reached by boat from below the castle, is a remarkable 14th-century hermitage (admission as for the castle).

A1068 on, passing (in 3 miles) the end of a road (B1338; right) to Alnmouth (1 mile).

Alnmouth, on the estuary of the Aln, is a pleasant small seaside resort with fine sands and an excellent golf course.

A1068 on to Lesbury (½ mile), then B1339 (right) through Longhoughton for 4 miles more; then by an unclassified road (right) to Howick (1 mile).

Howick is a small village in a wooded dene descending to the sea. The rebuilt church contains a monument to the second Earl Grey, promoter of the Reform Bill of 1832, who lived at Howick Hall which was built in 1782 and stands in delightful gardens (admission April to September, daily, 2 to 7), noted for their rhododendrons.

Unclassified road on to Dunstan (2 miles) where another road descends to Craster (½ mile).

Craster is an attractive fishing village with a small harbour, enclosed by fine cliff scenery. A footpath leads north along the coast for nearly 1½ miles to Dunstanburgh Castle (admission weekdays, 9.30 to 4, 5.30 or 7; Sundays from 2), begun in 1313 by Thomas, Earl of Lancaster, the opponent of Edward II. It stands on a basaltic cliff (an outcrop of the Great Whin Sill) and consists of a huge ward or bailey, enclosed by a long curtain wall, defended by towers and entered through the imposing gatehouse, converted into a keep about 1380 by John of Gaunt.

Unclassified road on (north) from Dunstan to Embleton (2 miles).

Embleton has a restored 13th-century church and a 14th-century fortified vicarage of the unique Northumbrian type.

B1339 on (north) for 1½ miles, then B1340 on again to Beadnell (4½ miles more).

Beadnell is a fishing village and small summer resort near the north end of Beadnell Bay, with its fine sands.

B1340 on to Seahouses (2 miles).

Seahouses, a fishing village with a busy harbour, is the port of embarkation (motor-boats daily in summer) for the Farne Islands, the easternmost outpost of the Great Whin Sill, an archipelago of about 30 small islands and rocks, lying between 1½ and 5 miles from the coast, and remarkable as a breeding place for sea-birds and grey seals. The best time for a visit is late May and early June, but during the nesting season only the Inner Farne and Staple Island are accessible. On the Inner Farne, which has cliffs up to 80 feet high, St. Cuthbert lived in solitude for eight years and he died here in 687. From the Longstone, the outermost of the larger islands, Grace Darling and her father, the lighthouse-keeper, set out to rescue the survivors of the ' Forfarshire ', wrecked in 1838.

B1340 on, skirting the extensive St. Aidan's Dunes, which command a fine view of the Farnes, to Bamburgh (3 miles).

Bamburgh, the Saxon capital of Northumbria from the 6th to the mid-8th century, is now a colourful village of stone cottages, round a wooded green. It is dominated by the magnificent castle (admission Easter-September, daily, 2 to 8), a royal fortress from Norman times to the reign of Henry VI, on an immense basaltic crag that shelters the village from the sea. The massive keep is a genuine Norman work of the 12th century; the state apartments were freely restored in the 18th century and again (more extensively) after 1894 for the 1st Lord Armstrong, the engineer. The fine church, at the upper end of the village, is mainly of the 13th century, with a vaulted crypt below the long chancel. In the churchyard is the ornate tomb of Grace Darling, the heroine of the Farne Islands, whose boat is preserved in the Memorial Museum opposite.

B1342 on (west) to Budle Bay (2 miles) and thence to Waren Mill (1 mile), then inland (left) for 2 miles more; then A1 (right) to Belford ($\frac{1}{2}$ mile).

Belford is an attractive small market town, once a coaching stage, on the Great North Road.

A1 on to West Mains ($6\frac{1}{2}$ miles) for the unclassified road descending (right) to Beal (1 mile), beyond which a causeway crosses the intervening sands (dry only from $3\frac{1}{2}$ hours after high tide to 2 hours before) to Holy Island (4 miles farther).

Holy Island, formerly Lindisfarne, was the cradle of Christianity in the North of England. Here St. Aidan, invited from Iona, in Scotland, by King Oswald, established a bishopric in 635, and here St. Cuthbert, made bishop in 684, was buried in 687, but the monastery was sacked during the first of the Danish raids on Britain, in 793. When the Danes attacked the island again, in 875, the monks escaped with the saint's body and after seven years of wandering settled at Chester-le-Street. Lindisfarne Priory (admission daily, 9.30 to 4, 5.30 or 7; closed Sundays in winter until 2) was refounded after 1081 for Benedictines. The beautiful red sandstone ruins comprise the 12th-century church, a remarkable example of Norman building, resembling the mother-house of Durham, and the fortified 13th-14th-century domestic buildings. A small museum contains carved stones from the Saxon monastery. The windswept fishing village called Holy Island, close by, has a 12th-13th-century church with a characteristic Northumbrian bell-cote. To the east, on a steep basaltic outcrop, rises the small Lindisfarne Castle (admission April-September, usually daily, except Tuesdays, 2 to 6), built about 1550 and much altered by Sir Edwin Lutyens.

A1 on from West Mains to Tweedmouth (7½ miles) and thence across the river to Berwick-upon-Tweed (½ mile).

Berwick-upon-Tweed is a fascinating port and fishing town on the north bank of the river, almost at its mouth. For over 300 years Berwick suffered from its position on the frontier between England and Scotland; it changed hands no fewer than 13 times between 1147 and 1482, when it was finally taken by the English. The 17th-century Old Bridge, the Royal Tweed Bridge, a concrete road bridge of 1928, and the long Royal Border Bridge of the railway, built by Robert Stephenson in 1847, all cross the Tweed. At the foot of Marygate is the 18th-century Town Hall, with a dominating steeple, and to the north of this is the parish church of 1652, one of the few built during the Commonwealth. The Scots Gate, at the head of Marygate, penetrates the Elizabethan ramparts, a system of fortification begun in 1558 and unique in Britain, but based on a plan first developed at Verona and Antwerp. They enclose a smaller area than the Edwardian town walls, of which only fragments remain. Of the castle, where Edward I gave judgement in 1292 in favour of the claims of John Baliol to the Scottish throne (see below), some walls survive to the west of the station.

A1 back over the river to Tweedmouth, then A698 (right) for 4½ miles and by an unclassified road (right) to Norham (3 miles).

Norham is an attractive village built round a spacious green and facing across the broad Tweed into Scotland. The impressive church, in which Edward I held a convention to decide between the claims of Bruce and Baliol, is partly Norman. To the east rise the beautiful pink-sandstone ruins of the castle (admission weekdays, 9.30 to 4, 5.30 or 7; Sundays from 2), the imposing Border stronghold of the prince-bishops of Durham from 1121, with a massive Norman keep and 12th-century walls. The castle was partly rebuilt after 1513, when James IV besieged it on his way to Flodden Field.

B6470 left (east) for ½ mile, then by an unclassified road (right) crossing A698 to Grindon (2 miles more) and on for 3 miles farther; then B6354 (right) to Etal (1 mile).

Etal is a charming village consisting of a street of white-washed cottages leading to the gatehouse-tower and keep of a 14th-century castle, near the Till.

B6354 on for 1½ miles, then B6353 on again to Ford (½ mile).

Ford is a model village laid out after 1859 by the Marchioness of Waterford, who also painted the water-colours of Scriptural scenes in the school. The restored 13th-century church has a characteristic bell-cote. The castle, farther west towards the Till, was partly rebuilt in the 18th and 19th centuries, but retains three of its original 14th-century corner towers.

B6353 on for 4 miles, then A6111 (right), with views of the Cheviot Hills, to Doddington (4½ miles more).

Doddington has a ruined pele-tower of 1584, one of the last Border towers to be built, and a 13th-century church with the chancel at the west end.

A6111 for 3 miles, then A697 (left), by-passing Wooler, described in Tour 10 (page 62) and on to Powburn (8½ miles).

Powburn lies south of the Breamish, the upper course of the Till. An unclassified road, on the west of the main road, 1 mile north, ascends the valley via Ingram (3 miles), which has an information centre for the Northumberland National Park, and ends nearly 3 miles farther on, short of the prehistoric village of Greaves Ash and the waterfall of Linhope Spout.

Unclassified road on from Powburn to Glanton (1½ miles) and thence to Whittingham (1½ miles more).

Whittingham, an attractive village on the Aln, has a restored 15th-century pele-tower and a much-rebuilt church with a Saxon tower.

Unclassified road right (south-west) to Callaly Castle (2 miles).

Callaly Castle, (admission June-September, Saturdays, Sundays and Bank Holidays, 2.15 to 6) below the wooded sandstone escarpment of Callaly Crags, consists of a pele-tower of 1415 or earlier, added to in the 17th and 18th centuries and altered in the 19th century.

Unclassified road on to Lorbottle (2½ miles), then left, skirting Rothbury Forest, to Thropton (3 miles more), on the Coquet; then B6341 (left again) to Rothbury (2 miles) and B6344 (right), passing the entrance to Cragside (1 mile more).

Rothbury, in a narrow part of Coquetdale, below the heather-covered moors of Rothbury Forest and backed on the south by the Simonside Hills (Tour 10), is a delightful market town with a wide grass-bordered main street. The much-rebuilt church has a font made from a fine carved Northumbrian cross of the 9th century, with a bowl dated 1664. Cragside is a rambling house built in 1870 by R. Norman Shaw for Lord Armstrong, the engineer, surrounded by beautiful grounds (admission Easter-September, daily, 10 to 8), best seen in June, when the rhododendrons are in bloom.

B6344 on through the dale to Brinkburn Priory (3 miles; on the right).

Brinkburn Priory (admission daily, 9.30 to 4, 5.30 or 7; closed Sunday mornings in winter), sequestered in the dale, was an Augustinian foundation of which the carefully restored late-12th-century church survives.

B6344 on to Weldon Bridge (2 miles), then A697 (right, over the Coquet) to Longhorsley (2½ miles more) and on for 4½ miles farther; then A1 (right) for ½ mile and by an unclassified road (right again) descending to Mitford (1 mile more).

Mitford is a scattered village charmingly situated in the wooded valley of the Wansbeck. Near the river, upstream, are the ruined 12th-13th-century castle and the restored 12th-13th-century church.

B6343 downstream to Morpeth (2 miles).

10. The Border Hills

This tour, starting from Alnwick, on the Great North Road, a delightful market town famous for its magnificent castle of the Percy family, Earls and Dukes of Northumberland, circumnavigates the Cheviot Hills, the range of wild, mountainous moorlands traversed by the border between England and Scotland. These quiet hills, with their steep and narrow valleys, are mostly covered by grass, though with occasional tracts of bracken and heather, and flocks of the black-faced Cheviot sheep graze on their slopes. From Alnwick the route crosses to the open middle section of Coquetdale and thence to Redesdale, which it ascends to cross the border at Carter Bar, the finest of the roads into Scotland. The tour takes in the old towns of Jedburgh (with its splendid abbey), Yetholm and Wooler; secluded villages like Elsdon, Harbottle, Kirknewton and Chillingham; and many fine Border castles, including that at Chillingham, standing in a beautiful park, where the only white wild cattle in England may be seen; as well as the battleground of Flodden Field and the lovely Hulne Park, near Alnwick.

Alnwick is an unspoilt stone market town, charmingly situated above the Aln. The 15th-century Hotspur Gate, at the south end, is the only survival of the medieval town walls. In the market place are the 18th-century Town Hall and the fine Northumberland Hall of 1826. The interesting 14th-15th-century church lies to the north-west, via Narrowgate and Bailiffgate. Alnwick Castle (admission May-September, Sunday to Thursday, 1 to 5), in a great park, has been since 1309 the chief stronghold of the influential Percys, of whom perhaps the most famous was Harry Percy, 'that Hotspur of the North' (son of the 1st Earl of Northumberland), killed at Shrewsbury in 1403. The castle is one of the most impressive medieval fortifications in England, though often restored and altered. The 12th-century curtain walls were strengthened by the 1st Lord Percy in 1309-15, when the towers were added. The outer bailey is entered through a formidable gatehouse of about 1440, defended by an imposing barbican; the inner ward is approached from the middle bailey by a gatehouse of about 1350. In the keep, largely rebuilt about 1764 for the 1st Duke of Northumberland, are the state rooms, mostly reconstructed in 1854-65 for the 4th Duke, who employed Italian artists and craftsmen to decorate them. They contain paintings by Italian and other masters and elaborate 18th-century French furniture, and in the library are many fine early manuscripts and printed books. The 14th-century Postern Tower, east of the keep, contains a collection of antiquities. The Berwick road crosses the Aln north of the castle by the Lion Bridge (by Robert Adam, 1773), surmounted by the stiff-tailed Percy lion; Malcolm's Cross, near the road over ½ mile farther north, marks the spot where Malcolm Canmore, King of Scotland, was slain in 1093.

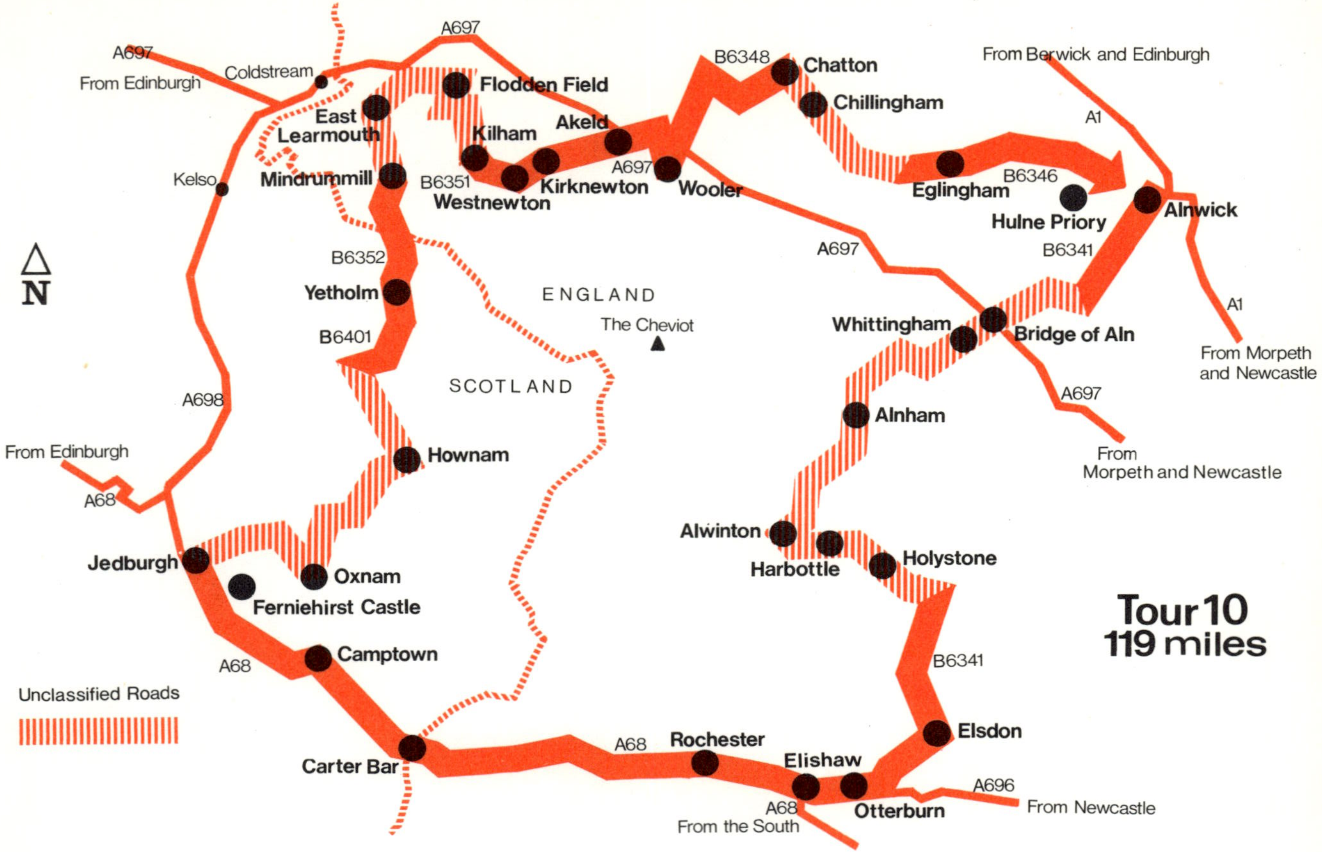

Tour 10
119 miles
Unclassified Roads
N
ENGLAND
SCOTLAND
The Cheviot
From Edinburgh
A697
Coldstream
A697
Flodden Field
East
Learmouth
Kilham
Akeld
Mindrummill
B6351
Westnewton
Kirknewton
A697
Wooler
Kelso
B6348
Chatton
Chillingham
Eglingham
B6346
Hulne Priory
Alnwick
From Berwick and Edinburgh
A1
A1
From Morpeth
and Newcastle
B6341
A697
Whittingham
Bridge of Aln
A697
From
Morpeth and Newcastle
Alnham
B6352
Yetholm
B6401
A698
From Edinburgh
A68
Hownam
Alwinton
Harbottle
Holystone
Jedburgh
Oxnam
Ferniehirst Castle
Camptown
A68
B6341
Elsdon
Carter Bar
A68
Rochester
Elishaw
Otterburn
A68
From the South
A696
From Newcastle

B6341 west from the market place for 3½ miles, crossing Alnwick Moor, with a fine distant view of the Cheviot Hills, then by an unclassified road (right) to Bridge of Aln (3½ miles more) and on to Whittingham (1½ miles).

Whittingham is described in Tour 9 (page 56).

Unclassified road on, branching right in 1 mile, to Eslington Hall, then right again via Great Ryle and Prendwick, with wide views to Rothbury Forest and Coquetdale, for Alnham (4½ miles more).

Alnham is a hamlet in a secluded valley under the southern flanks of the Cheviot Hills. It has a stout, late-medieval pele-tower (now a youth hostel) and a small late-12th-century church, poorly restored, with a typical Northumbrian bell-cote.

Unclassified road via Biddlestone Hall (3½ miles) and thence (right) to Alwinton (3 miles; to the right).

Alwinton, the highest village on the Coquet, lies below the point where the river emerges from a deep and narrow valley in the Cheviot Hills. A road, skirting the boundary of the extensive Redesdale Artillery Range, ascends the lonely upper section of Coquetdale as far as the farm of Fulhope (10 miles), 2½ miles below the Roman forts of Chew Green, on Dere Street, close to the Scottish border. From Fulhope another road (closed when the range is in use) crosses the moors to the south for Rochester (8½ miles; see below).

Unclassified road south from Alwinton, crossing the Coquet to Harbottle (1½ miles).

Harbottle, well situated below the moorland hills, has the fragments of a late-12th-century castle, with a fine motte and bailey.

Unclassified road on, branching right in 1½ miles, to Holystone (½ mile).

Holystone is a secluded hamlet facing across a wide bend of the Coquet to the Simonside Hills, a distinctive range of sandstone hills, profusely covered with heather and rising to 1447 feet in Tosson Hill. At the Lady's Well, reached from the inn by footpath, Paulinus is said to have baptized 3,000 Northumbrians in A.D. 627.

Unclassified road on, west of the Coquet, for 2½ miles, then B6341 (right) through a valley west of the Simonsides to Elsdon (5 miles farther).

Elsdon, built round a large green, has 18th-century and other old houses and a fine 14th-century church with unusual vaulted aisles (perhaps of the 17th century). Above it stands the embattled rectory or priest's house, built about 1400 and the finest example of this kind of fortification in the Border country.

B6341 on for 2½ miles, then A696 (right) to Otterburn (1 mile).

Otterburn, a small village in the broad Redesdale, is well known for the battle fought here in 1388, when the English, led by Harry Hotspur, who was captured, were defeated by the Scots under Douglas, who was killed. The encounter is the subject of the Scottish ballad of 'The Battle of Otterbourne' and the English ballad of 'Chevy Chase'.

A696 on to Elishaw (2 miles), then A68 on again to Rochester ($2\frac{1}{2}$ miles more).

Rochester is a remote hamlet with the 'last inn in England', in the wild valley of the Rede. Enclosing the farmstead of High Rochester, $\frac{1}{2}$ mile north, are the scanty remains of the Roman fort of *Bremenium*, which stood on Dere Street, the road (partly rebuilt by the army) crossing the moors to Chew Green (see page 59). Byrness (see below) is a village built by the Forestry Commission on the north side of the Border Forest Park (page 50).

A68 on to Byrness (5 miles) and thence to the Catcleugh Reservoir ($1\frac{1}{2}$ miles), then winding up from the head of Redesdale to Carter Bar (4 miles more).

Carter Bar, the site of 'The Raid of the Reidswire' (1575), celebrated in the last of the Border ballads, is the point (1370 feet) where this road from Newcastle to Edinburgh passes from England into Scotland (the finest of all the Border crossings). The magnificent view northward includes the Cheviot Hills, the Lammermuirs, the Eildon Hills and Ettrick Forest.

A68 on in zigzags down towards the valley of the Jed Water, which it crosses at Camptown (5 miles), then on above the glen, passing near Ferniehirst Castle (4 miles).

Ferniehirst Castle (now a youth hostel), the 16th-century stronghold of the Ker or Kerr family, stands in a charming wooded setting, above the east bank of the Jed Water.

A68 on to Jedburgh (2 miles).

Jedburgh, an attractive old town and a royal burgh, delightfully situated on the Jed Water, was mostly rebuilt after its destruction by the English in the 16th century. Facing the market place are the 18th-century New Gate, with the Town Steeple, and the former County Buildings, of 1812, where Sir Walter Scott made his first appearance as an advocate in 1793. To the east of the High Street is Queen Mary's House (admission weekdays April-October, 10 to 12, 1 to 5 and 6 to 8; Sundays 1 to 5 only), where Mary, Queen of Scots, stayed (and nearly died) in 1566, after her long ride to visit the Earl of Bothwell at Hermitage Castle. The 16th-century tower-house, of characteristically Scottish type, contains many interesting relics of the unhappy queen and her time. In Castlegate, to the south, Prince Charles Edward Stuart stayed at No. 11 in 1745, on his march into England. The castle, once an important royal fortress, was demolished in 1409 and its site is occupied by the county prison of 1823. To the south-east of the market place are the beautiful red sandstone ruins of Jedburgh Abbey (admission weekdays, 10 to 4 or, in April-September, to 7; Sundays from 2), founded in 1138 by David I for Augustinian canons, and much damaged by the English. The remains, mostly of the 12th and early 13th centuries, consist of the west front, with a fine late-Norman doorway, the long nave, the finest example of Transitional Norman work in Scotland, the tower, rebuilt in 1508, the truncated choir, and the transepts. The north transept contains a 15th-century chapel, the burial-place of the Kerrs, Marquesses of Lothian. The claustral buildings descend towards the river.

Unclassified road east, starting below the abbey, and crossing the hills bounding the Jed Water to Oxnam (4 miles).

Oxnam, in a secluded valley among low, green hills, on the west flanks of the Cheviots, has a church of 1738 with the iron jougs, or scold's bridle, on the outside wall.

Unclassified road left, passing near the church, then right, following a length of Dere Street on the way to Hownam (5½ miles).

Hownam is a remote village in the valley of the Kale Water, a haunt, in the 17th century, of the persecuted Covenanters.

Unclassified road down the valley, passing to the east of Morebattle (4 miles; see Letts Motor Tour Guide to *The Scottish Lowlands and Borders*), then right (east) to Primsidemill (2½ miles); then B6401 (right again) to Town Yetholm (1 mile).

Town Yetholm is a small town on the west side of the Bowmont Water, up which a road (from Primsidemill) runs to the sheep farm of Sourhope (6 miles), in the heart of the Cheviots. Kirk Yetholm, on the other side of the valley, was long the headquarters of the Scottish gipsy dynasty of the Faas. The last 'queen', Esther Faa Blyth, whose 'palace' is above the green, died in 1883. The character of Meg Merrilies, in Scott's *Guy Mannering,* is said to have been taken from an earlier 'queen'. Kirk Yetholm is at the northern end of the Pennine Way, the walking route from Edale, in Derbyshire.

B6352 on (north) from Town Yetholm, recrossing the border in 1½ miles, to Mindrummill (2½ miles more), then by an unclassified road on to East Learmouth (2½ miles) and for 1 mile farther, then A697 right for ¼ mile and by an unclassified road (right again) to Branxton (1½ miles), on the north side of the hill famous as Flodden Field.

Flodden Field is the site of the battle of 1513 in which the Scottish army under James IV, who had invaded England at the instigation of the French, was disastrously defeated by an English force led by the Earl of Surrey. A monument of 1910, 'To the Brave of Both Nations', marks the place where the king is believed to have fallen, mortally wounded.

Unclassified road (right), passing the Flodden memorial, for 1 mile, then left for 1 mile more and right for 1½ miles farther; then

B6352 (left) for ¼ mile and B6351 (right) via Kilham to Westnewton (2½ miles).

Westnewton is a hamlet at the foot of the beautiful valley of the College Burn, which rises on the west slopes of The Cheviot (2676 feet), the highest of the Cheviot Hills. A public road ascends the valley to Hethpool (1½ miles) and a private road (permits from the Estate Office, Wooler; see below) goes on thence to Mounthooly (4 miles farther), the highest farm.

B6351 on to Kirknewton (½ mile) and thence to Yeavering (1½ miles more).

Kirknewton, on the Glen, the lower course of the Bowmont Water (which flows from Scotland into England), has a church retaining a remarkable chancel and transept, of the 13th or early 14th century, with pointed tunnel vaults. At Yeavering, below the distinctive hill of Yeavering Bell (1182 feet), is the excavated site of a unique 7th-century palace of the kings of Northumbria.

B6351 on to Akeld (1½ miles), then A697 on again for 2 miles more and by an unclassified road (right) to Wooler (½ mile).

Wooler is an old-world market town at the north-east edge of the Cheviot Hills, and itself on a hill above the Wooler Water, the lower reach of the Harthope Burn, up which a road runs to Langleeford (5½ miles), below the east slopes of The Cheviot.

B6348 east (from A697), crossing the broad valley of the Till to Chatton (5 miles), then by an unclassified road (right) to Chillingham (1½ miles).

Chillingham has a 12th-13th-century church containing the magnificent tomb of Sir Ralph Grey, who died in 1443. The castle, built in the 14th century and altered about 1625, is enclosed by a fine park (open weekdays, except Tuesday, 10 to 5; Sundays, 2 to 5) in which roam the last wild cattle in England, whose kind have grazed here for over 700 years. The cattle are invariably pure white, and they are generally peaceable, but they should not be approached closely. Above the park rises Ros Castle (1036 feet), on the Great Whin Sill.

Unclassified road on for 2½ miles, then B6346 (left) to Eglingham (3½ miles more) and on, skirting Hulne Park (4½ miles farther).

Hulne Park is a large and beautifully wooded park, part of the Alnwick Castle estate (no cars admitted; permits for walkers required from the castle). Near the entrance is a fine 14th-century gatehouse, all that survives of Alnwick Abbey, and a footpath ascends for 1½ miles to the secluded 13th-century ruins of Hulne Priory, near the Aln, the best-preserved and perhaps the oldest example of a Carmelite friary in England. Brizlee Tower, beyond the river, commands a wide view to the Northumberland coast and the Cheviot Hills.

B6346 on over the river to Alnwick (2½ miles).

Index of Places

NORTHUMBERLAND AND DURHAM